Skating
Unrinked

Skating Unrinked

An Insider's Guide to Skating Trails in the San Francisco Bay Area

Richard Katz

HarperCollins*West*

A Division of HarperCollins*Publishers*

HarperCollins*West* and the author, in association with The Basic Foundation, a not-for-profit organization whose primary mission is reforestation, will facilitate the planting of two trees for every one tree used in the manufacture of this book.

FIRST EDITION

Katz, Richard

Skating unrinked : an insider's guide to skating trails in the San Francisco Bay area / Richard Katz. — 1st ed.

p. cm.

ISBN 0–06–258544–4

1. Roller-skating—California—San Francisco Bay Area—Guidebooks. 2. In-line skating—California—San Francisco Bay Area—Guidebooks. 3. Trails—California—San Francisco Bay Area—Guidebooks. 4. San Francisco Bay Area (Calif.)—Guidebooks. I. Title.

GV859.K38 1994

796.2'1—dc20   94–8441

CIP

94 95 96 97 98 RRD(H)   10 9 8 7 6 5 4 3 2 1

This edition is printed on acid-free paper that meets the American National Standards Institute Z39.48 Standard.

*Education is learning
from other people's mistakes;
experience is learning
from your own.*

Contents

San Francisco

South Bay

Points Beyond

Preface

When I was single I used to roller-skate in the streets quite a bit and didn't think much about dodging all the cars, buses, and pedestrians. It was fun, it was recreational, it was good exercise, and it was low impact, both on the environment and on the knees.

Some years later my wife, Clair, who was not much of a skater, encouraged me to find some safer and more enjoyable places to skate. When we went out as a family, it was important to be time efficient and to be mindful of the kids' safety. It was important to take the hassles out of skating.

So here is a guidebook for all the people who are intimidated by cars and love the out-of-doors. This is for people who have seen the skates in the store and wondered where they would go to do such a thing and also for all those people who bought their skates years ago and want to get them out of the closet.

About Places to Eat

For each of the trails in this book we have tried to steer you to one or two places nearby where skaters are welcome to eat. Out in Tiburon, we even found a place where skaters are "more than welcome"; it turns out the owner used to run a skate shop nearby. Skating is America's fastest-growing sport; at the current rate of growth, it seems like soon there will be two skaters per capita. Pretty soon nobody will find it the least bit odd when you skate into a restaurant to order lunch. Every place will be like Los Angeles's Venice Bike Path; not only is it a great place for family skating, but it's also socially acceptable to skate up to the counter at any establishment and order anything.

I'm from Point Richmond, and I've had ample opportunity to explore the phenomenological sociology of skating with the merchants in my own small town. At Little Louie's Deli it's no problem, you can skate on in; Edibles Cafe and Rosemary's Bakery, no problem; Little China, no problem for takeout. At the pizza place next to the old firehouse, on the other hand, you may be told that skating's not safe, that you might fall down and hurt yourself. An interesting middle ground is struck by the owner of the Santa Fe Market, who (if you are on skates) will go fetch your groceries while you wait by the door.

The embedded reasonableness of serving skaters was eloquently summed up at a sidewalk cafe table at Rosemary's Bakery by Rosemary's neighbor, a fellow by the name of McGowan: "I'm in the financial services business," he told me over coffee. "My stock in trade is that I'm reasonable. Why would I turn an investor away just because they've got wheels attached to their feet?" Thereby proving that he's a reasonable fellow indeed. In Port Costa, the other small town featured in this book, a fellow who runs the local landscape gardening shop across from the Warehouse Cafe told me that roller skates are okay with the Amish. I'm going to go back East someday and see if that's true, just go skating on some country road near Lancaster and see if the farmers wave like they do when you're on foot.

A Note About Equipment

Make sure the skates you use have 72 millimeter or bigger wheels. If they don't, you will get tripped up by sticks and stones lying in your path. If you do trip (and it happens to everybody eventually), **make sure you are wearing wrist-guards** and that you have practiced falling forward on them once or twice. Knee pads are nice, elbow pads are neat looking too, but bipeds like us need at a minimum something smooth and hard to fall on, something like the plastic insert in a good pair of wristguards.

If you're going out to play some hockey, wear the whole nine yards: gloves, elbow pads, knee pads, shin guards, a helmet, and a visor. And wristguards. And bring a stick.

Note: Remember, trail conditions can change. Always use your own common sense.

RK

Explanation of the
Rating System

Overall Rating

● An okay skating trail, especially if it is close to where you live.

●● A trail that has at least one feature nice enough to be worth stopping for a skate, if you're in the neighborhood.

●●● A trail with a number of interesting and pleasant features, worth going a bit out of your way for.

●●●● An outstanding trail, one you will want to return to many times.

●●●●● An exceptional skating experience, worth even a long trip, and not to be missed.

Path Surface

● Evaporated bumpy asphalt; concrete with severe expansion joints; or where plants are growing through surface.

●● Mildly bumpy asphalt; that is, asphalt with exposed aggregate (pebbles); concrete with thin expansion joints.

●●● Asphalt surface as good as a competently constructed roadway in good repair.

●●●● A new or fairly new asphalt path laid down by workers who knew they were constructing a path and not a road.

●●●●● A perfectly smooth surface, such as found at a roller rink or a freshly asphalted parking lot or the interior floors of a concrete warehouse. Need not be in perfect condition.

Public Transit Access

None It's in the middle of nowhere, and you can get there only with a car.

● It's pretty far from a bus stop or BART station, and the traffic is pretty intense.

●● It's pretty far from a bus stop or BART station, but the traffic is light.

●●● It's not too far from a bus stop or BART station.

●●●● It's next to a bus stop.

●●●●● It's next to a BART station.

Surroundings

Trails on city streets in unrelieved city environment, complete with car exhaust, didn't make it into this book.

● City environment; you may have to cross streets; noisy traffic.

●● No street crossings; surroundings may be pleasant, but you still have noisy traffic close by.

●●● Pleasant suburban surroundings without too much traffic noise.

●●●● Scenic surroundings with little traffic noise.

●●●●● Natural, beautiful, and quiet.

Level of Difficulty

Easy	Flat
Medium	Mild grades; nothing to be concerned about
Challenging	Grades in excess of 3 percent or more

Each trail includes portions appropriate for beginners. Most trails also include portions where experienced skaters can have some fun on grades or can visit interesting areas that require some street skating.

North Bay

Chapter 1

Skating in Sonoma

Ratings

Overall Rating	●●●
Path Surface	●●
Public Transit Access	●●●●
Surroundings	●●
Level of Difficulty	Easy
Length	2 miles one way

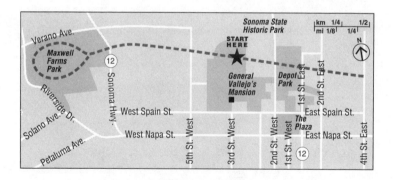

Sonoma is Disneyland without the rides or the hype. Its
magic is left over from the time when Costanoans, Spaniards,
Mexicans, Yankees, Sicilians, and Russians were sorting out
California. There's the mission, the fort, the plaza, the mansion,
the old train station, and the winery, as well as the place to
buy film.

Sonoma's recreation path runs east to west just north of the plaza for about two miles. You have to cross quite a few streets, but it's still okay for beginners. Park out toward the west end of town and skate on in. Downtown Sonoma can always use fewer cars.

How to Get There by Car

From northbound or southbound Highway 101, take the Vallejo/Highway 37 exit and go east on Highway 37. When you see large signs advertising drag races at Sears Point Raceway, get ready to turn left onto Highway 121 north. Several miles north on Highway 121, various signs direct you to the right turn onto Highway 12/121, toward Schellville and Sonoma. It's better to ignore the signs and continue straight north; the road eventually becomes Arnold Drive. About two miles past Leveroni Road, take the Petaluma Avenue fork slightly to the right (Arnold Drive veers left). After about a mile, Petaluma Avenue veers right and becomes West Napa Street. Go east on West Napa, then turn left on Third Street West. If you take this street to the end, you will be in General Vallejo's parking lot. You just passed the trail, which is a few hundred feet back.

What It's Like

General Mariano G. Vallejo had Northern California under his jurisdiction before the Gold Rush; he made a remarkable adaptation to United States hegemony. Starting at General Vallejo's place, you have the choice of going east to town or west toward Maxwell Farms Park. While you make up your mind, look around the general's house; his story is surprising, and it gives a historical overview for what you see around the town proper.

Start skating south from the mansion, around the pomelo trees until you get to the trail crossing. The pavement here isn't great, but it's adequate. This is the longest uninterrupted stretch you will see today. If you've decided to skate to town, turn left. After you cross First Street West, you will be skating through Depot Park, A Place of Importance to Visit in Sonoma, according to the sign. You can skate around a few old rail cars and inspect the station, which is also the Sonoma Valley Historical Society's Historical Museum. The trail passes next to Sebastiani Winery and ends at Fourth Street East. If you look around, you see the vestigial railroad near Sebastiani's; not too far east of town, on Eighth Street, you can see the end of the line of the real railroad, the Northwestern Pacific.

Start skating back toward Vallejo's place. During the week, when no hordes of tourists flood town, you may want to do a little street skating when you get to Second Street East. Turn left on Second, go one block, and get on the sidewalk to have a look at the restored Mission Solano on East Spain Street, between First East and Second East. This is where the Spanish missionaries rounded up the Indians and took them to die. Not a happy place.

The corner of First Street East and East Spain Street is the corner of Sonoma Plaza. What an incredible city block! Something unique is going on in just about every doorway. Skate over to the Toscano Hotel, a short way west on Spain Street, and peer into a place purposely frozen in time. Skate around the State Historic Park behind it. Skate through the plaza, and see the old library that was turned into a tourist info booth (among other things). Sonoma has so many eateries, bakeries, and stores of all stripes that it will take an hour just to check it all out. Be sure to skate to the other side of the plaza to study the mural of the plaza painted on a wall on Broadway. Find your way back to the path and skate west back to the general's house.

If you decide to skate west, you'll skate through backyards and a housing tract. Note the five-star pavement sometimes used for basketball in Olsen Park. The path seems to come to an end approaching Highway 12, the Sonoma Highway. Have faith; the trail reappears on the other side of the road. If you have small children, you might want to turn back here: Sonoma Highway is an officially designated State Scenic Route, but at this point it is more speedy and less scenic. To continue on, skate down to the crosswalk, the one they put in for the shopping center. There is a crosswalk button for those of us who aren't daredevils. Skate back up the street, and you will see some first-class pavement leading into the county's latest park, Maxwell Farms Regional Park. The whole trail is about two miles from downtown out to Maxwell Farms, with another half-mile loop around the park.

On your next trip, you might want to start at the park. Little kids really like the playground setup and the miniature golf course next door.

Places to Eat

Sonoma Plaza and its immediate environs (like East Napa Street, just off the plaza) have tons of places where you can eat well. Sonoma Cheese Company, for example, will pack picnic sandwiches for you.

On the way into town (or out of town, après-skate), stop at Angelo's, just south of the busy intersection where Highway 121 meets Arnold Drive. Try their smoked turkey and teriyaki jerky, and wash it down with cherry juice. Then go across the street to Gloria Ferrer's champagne caves. You can sit outside on what has to be the nicest back porch on earth. They like kids at Gloria Ferrer's and will feed them tasty smoked almonds while you drink champagne. And here's the great part: Schellville Aviation is across the street, so you can watch the vintage planes.

Public Transportation

There is daily service to Sonoma on Golden Gate Transit's 90 line. Only two buses depart each day from San Francisco, via San Rafael.

Other Trails to Check Out in the Neighborhood

On the way to Sonoma, check out the bike path at the Marin Civic Center. Take the North San Pedro Road exit in San Rafael from Highway 101 and follow the County Offices signs. The bike path is near the lake.

The skating facilities at the civic center aren't all that good. For example, the paved path at the big pond doesn't go all the way around (perhaps intentionally, so the pond would be a more meditative spot). All the trails are decrepit; after all, this place was built in the fifties and probably needs to be repaved. The real reason to come here is to spend a little time with Frank Lloyd Wright. The same outrageousness that brought us the spiraled Guggenheim Museum in New York brought us the Marin Civic Center. So stop in over the weekend to skate. Before you make the trip, though, make sure no big events are happening at the Marin Center or in any of the other meeting halls or theaters that share the grounds with the county administration building. Skate around the lower areas and Wright-designed parking lots; check out the *details*. Look up at that administration building. Amazing. Try not to notice that an extension being added to Wright's building looks like a jail.

Chapter 2

Stafford Lake Park to Novato

Ratings	
Overall Rating	●●
Path Surface	●●; some ●
Public Transit Access	●●●●
Surroundings	●●●
Level of Difficulty	Medium
Length	3 miles one way

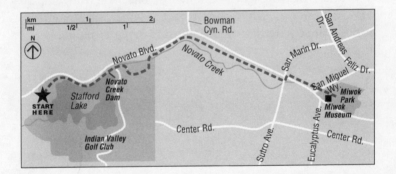

The path from Stafford Lake Park in upper Marin County to the San Marin district of Novato has an antique look and feel. It's narrow and it's old and it's cracked. But that's okay; it's still a good place to go out and skate, because it's out in dairy farm country, which is out of the ordinary for most of us.

At the beginning of the trail is a well-maintained county park with a resident flock of geese and a playground for kids. Picnic tables and lots of open space surround the reservoir.

There is a bit of traffic on the country road next to the trail.

Note: Bring four quarters along for the parking meters.

How to Get There by Car

From northbound or southbound Highway 101, take the Atherton Avenue/San Marin Drive exit. Go west on San Marin Drive; this is a six-lane road through a modern, slightly industrial district (note the suburban headquarters of Fireman's Fund Insurance on your right). At the intersection of San Marin and San Andreas is a big shopping center with a Petrini's, where you can buy picnic supplies or get your four quarters for parking. Gradually, the road shrinks to two lanes in each direction and hooks around to the south to meet up with Novato Boulevard. San Marin High School is on the right. Across the street is the end of the trail.

Make a right turn onto Novato Boulevard, heading west again. Punch your odometer. (You are now on Hicks Valley Road.) You will pass Bowman Canyon Road on the right leading to a quarry. After 2.4 miles, you will see a wooden sign on the left announcing Stafford Lake Park. Make the left turn, put your four quarters in the parking lot robot, turn left, and drive to the end of the parking lot. The trail begins on your right.

What It's Like

The trail quickly leaves lovely Stafford Lake Park, clinging to the edge of the lake as it runs back toward Stafford Lake Dam on your right. The first quarter mile of the trail is sinking back into the lake, so beware of longitudinal cracks and fissures. Although scenic, the path is on a rise, it's narrow, and it runs cheek by jowl to the highway on your left and a rickety wire-and-wood fence on your right. Skate with care.

At the end of a downhill slope followed by a blind curve is a stop sign for cars coming toward you from the right. Be wary of these motorists; they won't see you at all even though you think you've established eye contact with them. Let discretion be the better part of valor, and prepare to come to a full stop at the bottom of the hill. Make a right turn; the trail continues on your right behind a barred metal gate.

This part of the trail is also old and cracked, but it's very nice. At first it's a fair distance from the road, so the traffic noise abates somewhat. Then it meanders around a field for about a quarter of a mile. You might want to spend some time skating back and forth here, enjoying the cool, wooded, country atmosphere. Then it's back to the road again and a second barred metal gate and a trail that runs cheek by jowl to the highway.

This continues for a half mile or so, until you get to the T-shaped intersection with Bowman Canyon Road. There is a quarry at the end of that road, and the trucks leaving the quarry deposit a little bit of gravel each time they turn onto the highway. This makes the skating path nearly impassable here, but having been forewarned you can pick your way through it.

The trail hugs the side of the road for another mile. On the right is Neil O'Hair Park. The trail comes to an abrupt end at the intersection with Sutro Avenue, and I advise you to turn around here. However, experienced skaters could push on a little farther, past Sutro Avenue, skating on Novato Boulevard's bike path. The trail jogs to the north side of the street and runs into Miwok Park, where you can visit the Marin Museum of the American Indian. The tale of the Navajo Talkers in World War II is fascinating.

On the return trip, take a short detour to the left at the Indian Valley Golf Club sign. Cross Novato Creek on a

cracked concrete bridge and head left at the sign that directs
you to the North Marin Water District facility. They've created
a handsome outdoor display from a 24-inch-diameter steel
valve on a plinth. (Watch out for the cars from the golf
course.) Experienced skaters could climb the five-star pavement to the top of the dam for the beauty of the view as well
as the rush of the descent.

Places to Eat

Not even a water fountain can be found along this trail. If you
want a bite to eat, better buy it at the shopping center at the
corner of San Marin and San Andreas, and have a picnic at
the park while you stare at the cows across the road.

Public Transportation

You can get to the corner of San Marin Drive and Novato
Boulevard on the Golden Gate Transit 50 bus line. The corner
of Redwood Boulevard and Grant Avenue is a major transfer
point for Golden Gate Transit.

Other Trails to Check Out in the Neighborhood

Old Lucas Valley Road. Take Highway 101 south from Novato
to Lucas Valley Road. Head west on Lucas Valley Road about
one and a half miles to Mt. Lassen Drive; turn left onto Mt.
Lassen Drive and park anywhere. Old Lucas Valley Road runs
east. The old highway is now a Marin County open space
called Jerry K. Russom Park. Nature is encroaching on both
sides of this abandoned road, and it is now little more than a
horse trail in places. The county is doing a little work on it,
and perhaps in time it will be a better place to skate than it is
now. This trail is only about six-tenths of a mile long.

A little farther west on Lucas Valley Road, just across from the T-shaped intersection with Mt. Shasta Drive, is another isolated and abandoned section of Old Lucas Valley Road to skate on. And a little farther west, across from Mt. McKinley Road, is another section about four-tenths of a mile long. If you happen to be in this Marinwood neighborhood on the way to Point Reyes, check it out.

Chapter 3

The Cross Marin Trail

Ratings

Overall Rating	●●●●
Path Surface	●●; some ●●●
Public Transit Access	●●●● (but the service is infrequent)
Surroundings	●●●●
Level of Difficulty	Easy
Length	About 2 miles one way

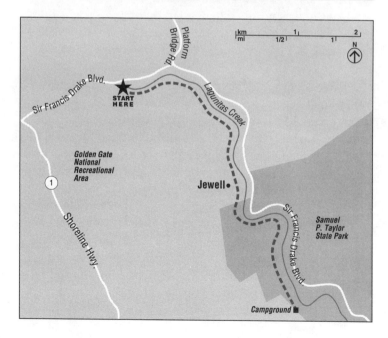

The Cross Marin Trail is an incredibly scenic roller-skating trail. Where else in the world can you roller-skate through over two miles of redwoods?

The Cross Marin Trail is partly in Samuel P. Taylor State Park and partly in the Golden Gate National Recreation Area. This trail is flat, level, smooth, and well maintained. Sir Francis Drake Boulevard runs parallel a few hundred feet away, so you'll hear some traffic noise. Plenty of free parking can be found at the western end of the trail.

How to Get There by Car

From northbound or southbound Highway 101, take the Sir Francis Drake Boulevard West exit in Larkspur. Head nearly 10 miles west on Sir Francis Drake, through Greenbrae, Kentfield, Ross, San Anselmo, Fairfax, Woodacre, and San Geronimo.

Punch your odometer to zero at the intersection of Sir Francis Drake and Nicasio Valley Road.

Continue west on Sir Francis Drake, through Forest Knolls and Lagunitas. The last stop for food and water is the Lagunitas Market, at the corner of Sir Francis Drake and Cintura Avenue.

There is a green metal bridge about 2.9 miles past Nicasio Valley Road. A concrete bridge follows at 4.1 miles. At 4.7 miles, on the left, is the campground and park headquarters for Samuel P. Taylor State Park. Continue on through the town of Jewell. At 7.8 miles, you will see a sign for Tocaloma and a road off to the right called Platform Bridge Road. Immediately after that, you will come to a concrete bridge and a brown sign that says Bike Path. Get ready to turn right into the driveway *just* past this bridge, where the sign says End 40 Mi. Zone. Take a quick left onto an abandoned concrete street, and park. Walk down the driveway toward the old concrete cantilever bridge. The trail entrance is through the underpass on your right. The level part of the trail starts on the other side of the underpass, so beginners need to walk down the first part of the trail and under the highway before putting on skates.

The entrance to the trail is marked by a sign saying Cross Marin Trail To Jewell Trail 1.4 Mi/To S P Taylor SP 3.5 Mi.

What It's Like

The path follows Paper Mill Creek (also known as Lagunitas Creek). Samuel P. Taylor built a paper mill and a black powder mill along this creek in the late 1800s; he also built a lake and a resort. The powder mill blew sky-high in 1874. The resort, though, was quite a place before Taylor went bust around the turn of the century. The path is built on the recycled roadbed of the former North Pacific Coast Railroad, which ran from Larkspur to Cazadero. Recreational camping was quite a novelty back then, and families would take the train to Camp Taylor to camp and picnic.

The path runs 1.5 miles to the intersection with Jewell Trail and then another 1.9 miles to the campgrounds of Samuel P. Taylor State Park. When you get to a closed gate made of logs, you'll see a pair of restrooms on your left. Don't explore the yellow and green metal bridge to your left; the boardwalk surface is treacherous. I suggest you turn around when you come to the campground, where the trail becomes a road (for another 0.5 miles on a rough surface before you get back to the highway). If you continue on the road through the campgrounds, you may have a problem with the campers and their automobiles, especially in the summer. This campground is generally full during good weather, and the cars roar in and out of camp as if they were on location for the *Road Warrior* movie.

Sometimes it takes a while for the park service to sweep the needles off the path after a rain. The asphalt is slightly rutted in places, as though several bicyclists plowed through it on a real hot day.

The Cross Marin Trail is on one of the standard bicycle routes from Point Reyes to San Francisco. Some of the bicyclists are moving fast, so keep to the right.

Places to Eat

There's no place along the trail to buy a snack, much less a meal. You could stop in San Anselmo on your way in and get a burger at Blimps, then go across the street for a good cup of coffee at Java del Porto, which is just off the main drag, past the movie theater and the Redwood Oil gas station. After skating, if you push on past the park, you can find food in Point Reyes Station. And remember the Lagunitas Market on Sir Francis Drake at Cintura Avenue. The market has an abundant variety of groceries and deli foods, serves espresso, and is open daily from 8 A.M. to 7 P.M.

Public Transportation

It's not easy, but you can get to Samuel P. Taylor State Park on the Larkspur Ferry and a Golden Gate Transit bus line.

During the week, the 24 bus line stops near the Larkspur Ferry dock. If you are a reasonably expert skater, you can strap your skates on and make the connection from the ferry dock to the Lucky Drive Bus Pad in about five minutes. Take a close look at the map of the Larkspur Trail System, and you'll see how it's done.

On weekends you have to get from the ferry to the 65 bus line; the route is somewhat byzantine and time consuming. A reasonably expert skater might consider skating from the ferry dock all the way over to downtown Larkspur, then out Magnolia Avenue to Bon Air Road, then out to Ross on the Corte Madera Creek Trail. The trail ends at Lagunitas Road in Ross, so you will have to skate on the streets and sidewalks of Ross and San Anselmo for a mile before catching the 65 bus as it plows through San Anselmo at Red Hill Avenue.

Other Trails to Check Out in the Neighborhood

The Trail System of Corte Madera and Larkspur

Chapter 4

The Trail System of Corte Madera and Larkspur

Ratings

Overall Rating	●●●
Path Surface	Mostly ●●● (but varies)
Public Transit Access	●●●●
Surroundings	●● (but great views)
Level of Difficulty	Easy
Length	About 2 miles each, one way

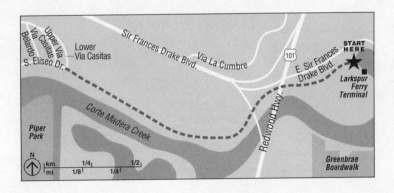

In the twin cities of Corte Madera and Larkspur (and extending into Kentfield and Ross) we have a system of not-quite-interconnecting paths that have one thing in common: you can look up at any time and drink in the skyline of Mount Tamalpais. Intrepid skaters can lace these paths into a synergistic whole with a bit of street skating; the more reasonable skaters among us can check these places out one by one.

Generally, the stretches of trail that run next to Corte Madera Creek are smooth and wide and suitable for beginners.

Larkspur Landing

How to Get There by Car

From northbound or southbound Highway 101, take the Sir Francis Drake Boulevard exit and turn east on Sir Francis Drake Boulevard. On your right you'll see the Larkspur Ferry and on your left the Larkspur Landing shopping center. There is a staging area just after the sculpture of Don Quixote on your right, across from Remillards Restaurant. Park here. If you get to San Quentin, you've gone too far.

What It's Like

Larkspur Landing (the part of Larkspur by the ferry dock) is the eastern terminus of this trail system. The first half mile runs from the ferry terminal along the south side of Sir Francis Drake Boulevard. But avoid the fumes by starting at the remarkable steel sculpture of Don Quixote. Continue skating west, past the Larkspur ferry docks and the antique shops, and under a railroad trestle. At the small, blue Downtown Larkspur sign, go left over a wooden bridge and boardwalk. This takes you under the freeway (very noisy) and onto a path with a very good asphalt surface leading to the shores of

Corte Madera Creek. Take the path to the left (the path to the right goes to Zim's Restaurant). Pass the Marin Rowing Association, and note the convenient outdoor soft drink vending machine. From here, the path continues about a mile, with the broad expanse of the creek to the left and well-tended industrial and residential condos to the right.

The path ends abruptly at a cul-de-sac on South Eliseo Drive. You can turn around here, or if you want to do some street skating and don't mind skating over a steep hill and down the other side, you can continue on South Eliseo about a half mile, and end up at:

Corte Madera Creek in Kentfield

How to Get There by Car

From northbound or southbound Highway 101, take the Sir Francis Drake Boulevard exit and go west on Sir Francis Drake Boulevard, past the Bon Air Shopping Center, to signs saying Bon Air Road and Marin General Hospital. Go left on Bon Air Road, at the churchlike structure on the corner. When you come to the End Divided Road sign, stop and park anywhere across from the hospital. Creekside Park is on the right.

What It's Like

Starting at Creekside Park, just west of an elegantly curved wooden bridge, skate west along the creek. (The wooden bridge takes you into downtown Larkspur, and even to Paradise Drive, the third of the trail systems we will explore in this chapter, but it's pretty rough sledding.) The first part of the trail goes by a par course, and there are mileage markers along the way. Soon you leave all the traffic noise behind, skating through marshland along the creek. Idyllic. With the sun setting over Mount Tam, it is—ineffable.

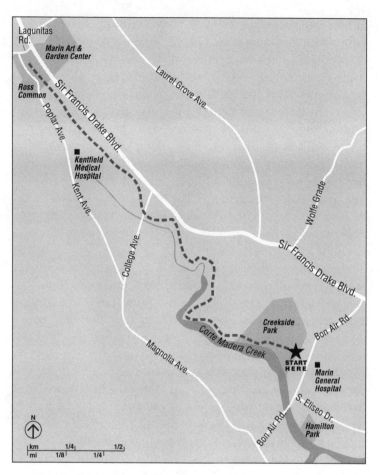

Corte Madera Creek was concreted in the sixties by the Army Corps of Engineers, much to the dismay of naturalists. They thought the area should be kept a floodplain, just in case a hundred-year flood occurs some time in the next hundred years. You'll notice that the creek gets more constricted the farther west you skate. By the time you cross the first wooden bridge, you'll wonder where all the water went.

There is a not-so-easy crosswalk to negotiate at College Avenue in Kentfield. A Guatemalan-flavored *taqueria* is over to your right a block. The path seems to end when you cross the street, but skate to the right of the kiosk, staying between the tin building and the brick retaining walls. Follow the Bike Route sign and bear left into the parking lot. Go around the boarded-up old "temporary" buildings to the triangular corner of the rough pavement in the parking lot. Look for the Bike Trail sign in the distance. The trail is now a narrow path by the creek. It goes up to street level on a wooden walkway at Kentfield Medical Hospital and comes to an end around the two-mile mark at Ross Common.

You can continue, if you don't mind some street skating. Skate to Lagunitas Road, turn right, cross Sir Francis Drake, and take a turn around the grounds of the Marin Art and Garden Center. Be careful around Ross Common, though. They don't have postal deliveries in Ross; everybody drives to the post office for mail, and it can get pretty crazy and congested.

If you want to skate some more after skating all the way back to Larkspur Landing, you can follow the little blue sign that says To Lucky Drive, just after you cross under the freeway skating east. It will take you over Corte Madera Creek to the Paradise Drive trails. (Note: It is easier and safer to get there by car.) Once you are on the south side of the creek, follow alongside the freeway on Redwood Highway, which at this point is mostly an odd succession of parking lots. (Note the pedestrian overpass; if you can negotiate that overpass successfully, you will find another trail on the other side that runs diagonally past Redwood High.) Past the shopping center with the Cost Plus store, on the left side of the road going south, you will see the beginning of a very unassuming skating trail:

Paradise Drive in Corte Madera

How to Get There by Car

Going northbound or southbound, exit Highway 101 in Corte Madera at the Paradise Drive/Tamalpais Drive exit and turn east on Paradise Drive. Nordstrom's Village is on your left. Continue on Paradise Drive and turn left at a T-like intersection onto Redwood Highway, the street closest to the marshlands. When the road makes a lazy turn and you see lots of open space on the right, park anywhere. You're in the middle of the trail, toward the northern end of it.

What It's Like

This trail goes south for a few miles, first on Redwood Highway and then continuing on San Clemente Drive, which runs into Paradise Drive. At the south end of Nordstrom's Village, you are skating just a few feet from a state ecological reserve. Paradise Drive soon runs out of steam as a place to skate, but someday take a drive along it all the way to the end, as it meanders majestically all around the Tiburon Peninsula.

Places to Eat

Where the Creekside Park trail crosses College Avenue in Kentfield, you can find three or four interesting places to get fed. Kentfield is a college town, sort of, with an eclectic group of restaurants. There's the Half Day Cafe, Nana's Cafe, the seafood restaurant, and even the healthy Local Yoghurt shop (which says Spacekraft Skateboard Co. on the door). The one that's okay to skate into is the Taqueria Mexican Grill, on the west side of College near Sir Francis Drake. Great burritos, and a little different; their motto is "If you're hungry and in a hurry." It's open every day.

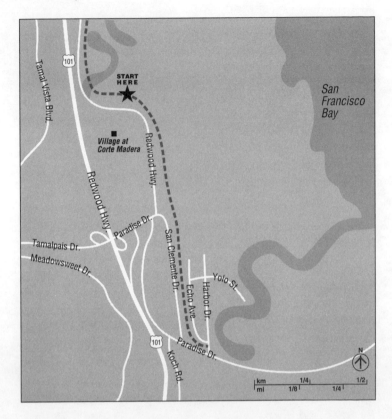

The elegant Nordstrom's Village has an entire enclosed mini-mall of small eateries, including a Starbucks and, just across from it, a bakery. And they're not bad. Nordstrom's Village is at the eastern end of Tamalpais Drive in Corte Madera.

Places to Rent Skates

Try Any Mountain (415-927-0170), open seven days a week. It's in Corte Madera, near Redwood High.

Public Transportation

Larkspur Landing is served by the Golden Gate Transit's Larkspur Ferry. The ferry dock is a major terminal where you can catch the Golden Gate 1 and 30 bus lines.

To get to the Ross end of the trail system, take the Golden Gate Transit 20 line. It will take you to College of Marin, for example.

All of these services operate daily. The 20 and 30 both go to San Francisco.

Other Trails to Check Out in the Neighborhood

Tiburon Multi-Use Pathway
Mill Valley to Sausalito

Note: Larkspur Ordinance 650 says No Rollerskating on the Sidewalk, as posted near Creekside Park.

Chapter 5

Mill Valley to Sausalito

Ratings

Overall Rating	●●
Path Surface	●●●
Public Transit Access	●●●●
Surroundings	●●●
Level of Difficulty	Easy
Length	2.5 miles one way

The Rails to Trails Conservancy is a nonprofit organization that recycles the roadbed of redundant or defunct railroads into skating, hiking, and biking trails. The results are a mixed bag; sometimes the reason that the railroad company abandoned the line is also a good reason not to want to skate there (if the way is too hemmed in by houses and grade crossings, for example). But sometimes the recycled roadbed provides a fine skating trail. This trail, the Mill Valley/Sausalito Multi-Use Pathway, succeeds because without the roadbed it wouldn't have been built. You couldn't, nowadays, just clear a path through a marsh and pave it over for humans. But by repaving the old railroad here, Rails to Trails has provided the unique opportunity to skate alongside the shorebirds.

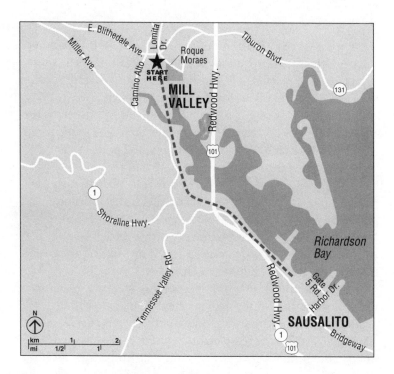

How to Get There by Car

From Highway 101 southbound, take the Tiburon/East Blithedale/Highway 131 exit. Stay to the right on the off-ramp, and turn right onto East Blithedale, following the Mill Valley Next Exit sign.

From Highway 101 northbound, take the Tiburon/Mill Valley exit, and turn left at the top of the off-ramp.

You will know you are on the right road when you see the Nuclear Weapon Free Zone sign. Stay to the left and cross the intersection of Lomita Drive (the first stoplight), then hang a U-turn at Camino Alto (the second stoplight). The skating trail is on the other side of the one-story office building that's on your right.

What It's Like

Except for three or four bumpy wooden bridges, this path is all smooth asphalt. In some places the asphalt is a little more evaporated than in others, but not badly. Start skating south where the trail heads across the marsh, near the corner of Roque Moraes Drive and East Blithedale. (Roque Moraes is the continuation of Lomita.) After a long stretch, you come to the Bay Front Park sign. Watch your step on the first wooden bridge near the traffic circle at the park entrance.

Investigate the interesting short trail to the left, near the traffic circle. In fact, at several places along this multi-use pathway you will see trails that veer off (all to the right, except for this one), and each one is worth a look. The trail that winds around the condos just up ahead on your right curves a long way along the public shoreline.

The first mile of this trail is especially pleasant, because there is no traffic nearby. Where the trail starts to run up against Shoreline Highway, you will notice some noise. Thankfully, the path cuts diagonally back across the quiet marshland for another half mile and then goes under an immense freeway overpass. From this point on, you are skating next to the road, accompanied by noise.

On the other side of the underpass is a stop sign. The trail continues, but take a minute here to turn left into the parking lot and head toward the big gray buildings labeled Shoreline Office Center. Behind the office complex is a public shore, more suitable for walking than skating, but if you go around the back of Building A (the one with the Leasing sign on it) you can skate to a particularly scenic panorama of the marshes and shoreline of Richardson Bay.

Returning to the stop sign, the trail continues past the houseboats of Sausalito and then becomes somewhat of a glorified sidewalk along Bridgeway. You might think about turning around here. This is the Silicon Valley of Sausalito (software companies, mostly), but there are a fair number of artists. Check out the IBC artists' complex, a huge hump-backed building down by the shore, with studios open to the public in early December.

Along this stretch you can see the vestigial railroad on your left going south. This whole area—the not-so-touristy part of Sausalito, with street names like Gate 5 Road—was a huge maritime industrial complex that turned out dozens of Liberty ships and Victory ships during the Great War. At Fort Mason in San Francisco you can gaze up from the waterline to the bow of the Liberty ship SS *Jeremiah O'Brien* and then eye-ball her from stem to stern. Here at Sausalito, down by Marin-ship Way, that immense vessel was forged from pipes and plates of steel and then launched near that fuel dock. Seems like a dream.

Places to Eat

You can grab a bite to eat at several places near the southern end of the trail along Bridgeway Boulevard in Sausalito. The supermarket over by the post office at Harbor Drive even houses a good deli counter.

Cafe Renoir (415-332-8668) is behind Building A of the Shoreline Office Center at 100 Shoreline Highway. When you skate south from the freeway overpass, go up the driveway at the stop sign, take a left, and look to the right of the flagpole. There is a wide wooden walk around the building, and in the corner where the outdoor tables are set up, facing Richardson Bay, is the cafe. No doubt you remember *The Boating Party,* by Pierre-Auguste Renoir. When you sit on the patio of the cafe, you're there. Lends a whole new meaning to the word *picturesque.* The good news is that it's open early in the morn-ing. The bad news is that it's closed on weekends. This white-tablecloth establishment always has a few very fresh sandwiches ready to go.

Public Transportation

Golden Gate Transit's 10 bus line stops at the north end of
the trail. You can catch the 10 bus at the Tiburon Ferry, at the
Sausalito Ferry, and in San Francisco at the Transbay Terminal,
along Howard Street or Folsom Street between First and Seventh Streets, along Van Ness Avenue, or on Lombard Street.

Other Trails to Check Out in the Neighborhood

The Trail System of Corte Madera and Larkspur

Chapter 6

Tiburon Multi-Use Pathway

Ratings	
Overall Rating	●●●
Path Surface	●●●; some ●●●● (near McKegney Green); some ●●●●● (past the ferry dock)
Public Transit Access	●●●●
Surroundings	●●
Level of Difficulty	Medium (traffic)
Length	2.5 miles

The Tiburon Trail starts in an estuary—one of the few official shoreline mudflats I have ever seen—and ends in one of the most pleasant shopping locations in the Bay Area. Tiburon is a great destination for an outing.

You can find free parking at the western end of the two-and-a-half-mile-long trail. The parking lot is unpaved, but the locals are respectful enough to drive slowly and not raise any unpleasant clouds of dust. At the other end of the trail, in the heart of town, parking spaces are at a premium.

The western part of the trail has no cross traffic and is especially inviting for kids and beginners. It does have one little slope near the parking lot.

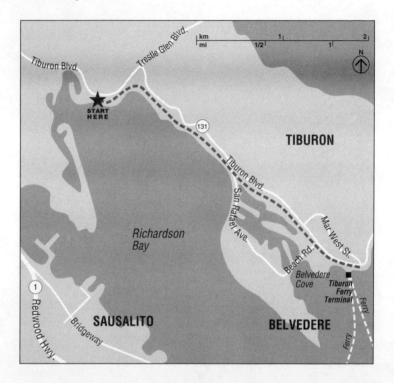

How to Get There by Car

From Highway 101 southbound, take the Tiburon/East Blithedale/Highway 131 exit. Stay to the left on the off-ramp, and turn left onto Tiburon Boulevard. (The same road is called East Blithedale on the other side of the freeway.)

From Highway 101 northbound, take the Tiburon/Mill Valley exit, and turn right at the top of the off-ramp.

Punch your odometer at the Chevron station, and proceed east 1.3 miles to the Blackie's Pasture Road sign. Make an immediate right. Drive slowly (so as not to raise a cloud of dust and disturb the locals) to the very back of the unpaved parking lot. The farther back you can get, the better; dust is the enemy of your wheel bearings. In fact, if you can park all the way to the back and to the right, you will be at the abandoned end of Greenwood Beach, at the western terminus of the trail.

You will know you are in the right place when you see a green street sign that says Bernini Way. Start skating east on the path, as indicated by that sign. Make sure you don't skate down the short path after the parking lot; it heads back toward Tiburon Boulevard and isn't much fun at all. Skate in the uphill direction.

What It's Like

This two-and-a-half-mile path follows the shoreline of Richardson Bay. After a short, slightly uphill section, there is a sharp left and then a right; keep heading east (and ignore that other little trail that beckons with a second left). The trail winds past McKegney Green, where on Sundays the teams of Tiburon play soccer until 1 P.M., when they must relinquish the field to sunbathers and newspaper readers. Stop at the wooden benches and enjoy the scenic overlooks. This section of the path is a beautiful stretch of very smooth pavement.

After McKegney Green, you skate through a genuine wildlife sanctuary, maintained by the Richardson Bay Sanitation District. The sanctuary has been officially dedicated with a bronze plaque fastened to a boulder by the side of the path, embossed with the likeness of a local sanitation engineer, Max H. Graefe, and the bon mot "Life Is Eternal." On the shore side of the trail are mudflats. On the landward side are the Richardson Bay Wildlife Ponds. Take the time to read and ponder the public service announcements framed in rustic lumber; they implore you to appreciate Nature, in large letters, while you are there. The primitive and inarticulate little creatures of Richardson Bay's briny swamp will turn that sign into food as soon as it gets too close to the benthic ooze of their flats.

There is no traffic on this stretch of the trail, and the distance is very clearly marked in quarter miles from either end.

Once you get to San Rafael Avenue the trail is a bit less idyllic, because you have to cross a street and then negotiate a boardwalk. You are now running parallel and next to the highway. Traffic noise can be intense at rush hour.

You will find another street crossing at Mar West Street. On the other side a sign clearly announces No Bikes. Do not fear. The Tiburon police say that skates are allowed everywhere in town.

As you approach downtown Tiburon, the remainder of the trail is less of a trail than a bike route.

When you get to a traffic circle, the trail is at an official end. Note that east of the traffic circle is a path along the water, once again lovely and scenic just as it was back by McKegney Green and the wildlife ponds. According to the Tiburon police, you may skate on that trail, right next to the bay. It's an unusual surface, made of a solid five-sack concrete with pea gravel exposed aggregate, which produces a remarkably smooth, hard surface with a good grip. Not only that, it's lighted at night. Bicycles are clearly instructed to use the bike lane in the street.

Places to Eat

You can find, of course, any number of sophisticated and palate-pleasing establishments in the worldly but laid-back town of Tiburon. Within a few yards of the roundabout are four or five excellent places to enjoy a meal or a snack. But for a party of skaters, there is only one place to go for food, drink, and rest, and that place is Paradise (415-435-8823). The owner of Paradise ran a skate shop up the street a few years ago. He still has a dozen beat-up pairs of rental skates in the back of the grill. And at Paradise, skaters are not just tolerated or

merely welcome; at Paradise, skaters are "more than welcome." Mr. DeSimone's bill of fare features zucchini sticks,
curly french fries, fresh salads, sandwiches, hamburgers, and
generous servings of ice cream. The address is 1694 Tiburon
Boulevard, right on the main drag.

Public Transportation

Tiburon has its own ferry dock—two of them, in fact. Golden
Gate Ferry goes to San Francisco and Sausalito and is a wonderful way to visit Tiburon. (You can't wear skates on the ferries.) The other ferry is run by the park service and goes to
Angel Island. Angel Island is a nice place to visit, but I
wouldn't want to skate there; the surfaces are rough.

The Golden Gate Transit 10 bus line serves Tiburon every
day; it stops at the Tiburon Ferry, the Sausalito Ferry, and
downtown San Francisco. The 8, 9, 11, and 45 also run during
commute hours.

Other Trails to Check Out in the Neighborhood

Mill Valley to Sausalito

East Bay

Chapter 7

Port Costa to Martinez

Ratings

Overall Rating	●●●●
Path Surface	●●● (watch for washout)
Public Transit Access	●● (Amtrak)
Surroundings	●●●●●
Level of Difficulty	Challenging
Length	5 miles one way

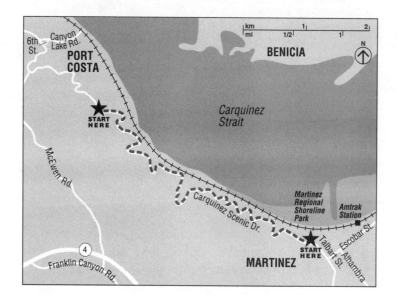

Carquinez Scenic Drive used to be a well-traveled thoroughfare between Martinez and Crockett. Then sometime during
the 1980s part of the road fell down the cliff and was never
repaired. Later in the decade, the East Bay Regional Park District acquired large tracts of land on both sides of the road—
land that has become Carquinez Strait Regional Shoreline.
This leaves the road, Carquinez Scenic Drive, in a unique situ-
ation: it's still there, it's got a good surface, it's got no through
traffic (in one section there's no traffic at all), it's easy to get
to, and for over four miles the view is, without exaggeration,
breathtaking.

Be forewarned, though: Carquinez Scenic Drive is not flat,
not straight, and for a short stretch, not all there. It's not for
beginners.

How to Get There by Car

From northbound or southbound Interstate 80, take the Her-
cules/Martinez exit to Highway 4 going east. Highway 4 is the
John Muir Parkway, but this part of it is usually called Highway 4 or Franklin Canyon Road. (Somehow John Muir just
never did catch on as a name for a freeway.)

Here, you have to decide if you want to approach the trail
from the west, near Port Costa, or from the east, near Martinez. After you read this chapter, you'll know which route is
more your cup of tea.

To start from the Port Costa side, take the McEwen
Road/Port Costa exit from Highway 4, go left under the freeway, and head north on McEwen Road. This is a twisting two-
lane road through unpopulated country. When you get to
Carquinez Scenic Drive, turn right. Not far from this intersection, you will come to a sign that reads Stop—Road Closed to
Martinez. You'll see a parking area on the north side of the
road, but don't park there! It belongs to Port Costa Materials
(a manufacturer of drainpipes), and they don't want anyone

in their parking area. Park, believe it or not, on the south side of the road, facing the Road Closed sign.

To start from the Martinez side, take the Alhambra Avenue exit from Highway 4, go left under the freeway, and drive into downtown Martinez. Turn left onto Escobar Street, then right onto Talbart Street. Just before Talbart Street disappears, Carquinez Scenic Drive heads off to the left. Less than half a mile west on the south side of Carquinez Scenic Drive, you will see the John A. Nejedly Staging Area, operated by the East Bay Regional Park District. Now you have to decide whether you wish to drive farther, perhaps as far as the Road Closed sign several miles down the road, or whether you would prefer to stop here and skate those several miles.

What It's Like

If you have come to Martinez and have arrived at the Nejedly Staging Area, put on your skates in the parking lot and head left on Carquinez Scenic Drive. There is rarely any traffic here. This road is open to the public, but it is largely unused. Occasionally, one of the locals will putt out to the drive to drink a beer or look at the river. The only other people you are likely to see are dog owners walking their pets, and bicyclists.

This road is full-sized, two-lane blacktop, and it goes along for two miles or so with many switchbacks and ups and downs. The views are already spectacular, and you haven't even gotten to the good part yet. After a particularly deep switchback near the Ozol tank farm (where the Air Force stores its fuel), you will come to a Road Narrows sign and, later, an eastward-facing Hazardous Area sign. You might consider turning around here; you have already skated over three miles.

If you have parked your car at the Road Closed sign on the Port Costa side, put on your skates and head east past the bullet-riddled sign. The conveyor belt overhead drops quite a bit of dirt on this section of road, but it's confined to a small strip. After about a mile of skating, with spectacular views of Carquinez Strait and the Sacramento River, you will be confronted by a westward-facing Hazardous Area sign. Step over the heavy iron gates that keep the cars out and make life difficult for the many bicyclists who use this path daily. About 200 yards past this gate you will come to the washout that closed this road to the public over a decade ago. Be careful: at one point, the surface is only a few feet wide (which lends new meaning to the sign Road Narrows). Not too far past this parlous crossing, you must traverse twenty feet of packed earth. If this sounds like a bit much, bear two things in mind: the view is well worth it, and if this road weren't damaged beyond repair you wouldn't be able to skate on it.

This path is definitely not flat.

Places to Eat

If you are on the Port Costa side of Carquinez Scenic Drive, you can go back to Port Costa, eat at the Warehouse Cafe, and generally hang out in Port Costa. To get there, return to the intersection of Carquinez Scenic Drive and McEwen Road, but continue on Carquinez Scenic Drive about a half mile until you come to an intersection with a very sharp right turn. Take the road that goes 120 degrees or so to the right, called Canyon Lake Road. After a few very scenic blocks, Canyon Lake Road comes to a picturesque end at the Sacramento River. Park anywhere. Port Costa is the little town at the end of the road. There isn't much happening, so feel free to skate around town and get acquainted. Note the remarkable sculptures along Canyon Lake across from the defunct Port Costa School.

The true oddity and charm of this place do not become apparent until you notice the sublime dichotomy of the Warehouse Cafe on one side of the street and the Bull Valley

Restaurant on the other. The Bull Valley (510-787-2244) is expensive and always packed; reservations are a good idea. The food is legendary. The Warehouse Cafe, on the other hand, serves beer in Mason jars. They have a monstrous stuffed polar bear in a glass case. They offer free lunches on Sundays if you buy a drink. They serve skaters. "Hell," says the bartender, "we serve anybody." Later on Sunday afternoons the Harley owners arrive. It's interesting, and although it may seem forbidding, trust me: it's a wonderful place to take your family.

Public Transportation

There is apparently no scheduled public transportation to Port Costa.

One can get to Martinez on the grandest and most public conveyance of all, the train. The telephone number of the Martinez Amtrak Station is 510-228-4008. This is a good number to know. No matter where you are in the United States, you can call this number and get accurate information about train arrivals and departures. The station agents in Martinez are all business. They will tell you when to be in Emeryville to catch the train to Martinez and when to be back in the station so you'll be returned home the same day. To get to the Nejedly Staging Area from the Martinez Amtrak Station, go south on Ferry Street, right on Escobar Street, and right on Talbart Street.

Martinez has some bus service (County Connection 108 and 116) but none on Sundays.

Other Trails to Check Out in the Neighborhood

The Contra Costa Canal
Ygnacio Canal Trail (see page 62)

Chapter 8

Point Pinole

Ratings

Overall Rating	●●●●
Path Surface	●●●
Public Transit Access	●●●●
Surroundings	●●●●●
Level of Difficulty	Medium
Length	About 2.5 miles one way

Before Hercules and Pinole became the fastest-growing twin cities in the United States, their promontory on San Francisco Bay's shoreline housed a little company town that manufactured explosives. As seventy-three-year-old Bill Thatcher told reporter Ed Kountz for the *West County Times* (December 7, 1993), "Every time there was an explosion, our house jumped a little further out of shape. It began to look like a cardboard box that was losing its shape."

The skating trail in East Bay Regional Park District's Point Pinole Regional Park runs through the former Giant Powder Works for over two miles. The trail has some ups and downs that make it a challenge for beginners. It's fun to try to decipher the lay of the land here—that is, to infer from the surviving landscaping how the former dynamite plant operated. Generally, a flat gravel path used to be the site of a narrow-gauge railroad (which was shipped off to Disneyland); the elegance of the palm trees signified company offices; the

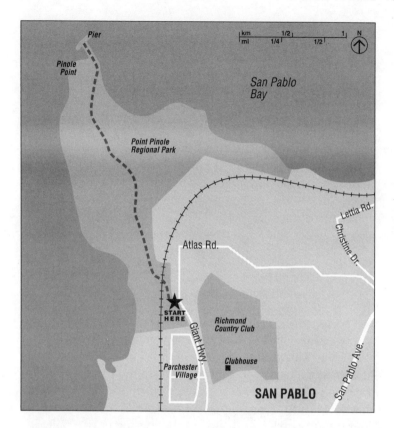

hedgerows of eucalyptus trees were planted to force the explosions up instead of out; and the general expansiveness of the layout kept the product segregated in different "houses" at various stages of manufacture, spread over a matter of acres. The craters—well, they speak for themselves.

How to Get There by Car

From eastbound or westbound Interstate 580, just before (westbound) or after (eastbound) the Richmond/San Rafael Bridge, take the Castro Street/Point Richmond exit. At the bottom of the off-ramp, turn north onto Castro Street. You're going the right way if you pass Chevron's huge refinery complex. Watch for the sharp right turn after the railroad tracks. Continue on to the first left turn, onto Richmond Parkway. (Note: This is a new road, only partially completed.) Take Richmond Parkway north and follow it as it curves right just after the new water reclamation plant. You are now heading east on the former Parr Boulevard. After you cross the Santa Fe Railroad tracks, take a left on Giant Highway. Go north on Giant, past the Richmond Country Club and Parchester Village, until you see the Point Pinole Regional Shoreline sign on your left. Turn left, go down a winding approach road, and park in the lot. On warm weekends, they charge for parking.

What It's Like

A serious iron gate at the western end of the parking lot keeps cars off the trail. From the moment you get your skates on and head through the turnstile, you won't have to worry about your kids getting run over or plowing into parked cars. After taking a turn or two just for fun around the circular drive on the other side of the gate, head up the slight incline that parallels the railroad tracks, on either of the two paths to your right. Skate left at the top of the rise and cross a railroad bridge. The trail at this point is a single-lane road called Pinole Point Road, and it heads generally north.

After you pass the children's playground and two picnic areas, you'll skate through about a mile of flat trail, then a right curve, a left curve, and a fairly steep downhill. This must have been one of those protected areas, maybe good for nitroglycerin packaging. You will come to a roundabout that looks remarkably like a bus stop; the park service runs a tram out here for older folks who want to go fishing. The fishing pier on the other side of the bus stop area is a nice long skate in itself, and the engineers took the time and trouble to specify rubber expansion joints in the crosswise direction, so you can skate all the way down without a problem. In-line skates might catch a divot on the lengthwise joints, though, so avoid the crack running down the center. There's plenty of room to turn around at the end and head back. This pier is a marvelous place for observing the shore from a half mile out to sea. Just watch out for the anglers and their monofilament.

Places to Eat

After you exit the freeway on the way to Point Pinole, there is no place to buy food or drink. If you want to pick something up, the last stop is in Point Richmond, around the bend from the bottom of the ramp off Interstate 580.

If you want to grab a quick meal after you skate, head back out to Giant Highway and go left, past the jail, and follow what is now Atlas Road past Marwais Steel and UPS to the intersection with San Pablo Avenue. Take a left on San Pablo, and after about a mile you'll see the Tara Hills shopping center. On the far side of the parking lot is a Mexican restaurant called Taqueria Morelia No. 2; the food is real tasty and reasonably priced. (Taqueria Morelia No. 1 is a cantina down in Oakland, on East 14th Street near High Street, and it's just as good.)

Public Transportation

AC Transit's 78 bus line stops at the park on its way to the West County Jail. You can catch the 78 at Richmond BART. And you can get to Richmond BART from Amtrak just by crossing under the tracks!

Other Trails to Check Out in the Neighborhood

Miller-Knox Regional Park in Point Richmond

Chapter 9

Miller-Knox Regional Park in Point Richmond

Ratings	
Overall Rating	●●●●
Path Surface	Mostly ●●; some ●●●; figure-skating/roller hockey pad is ●●●●●
Public Transit Access	●●●●
Surroundings	●●●●
Level of Difficulty	Easy
Length	A loop of about 1 mile

Along the shore of a duck pond constructed on a former railroad yard at Ferry Point lies a one-mile path that's as close as you'll find to an outdoor roller rink—flat, level, smooth, and fairly well maintained. The pond, the trail, and the surrounding picnic areas are part of Miller-Knox Regional Shoreline Park, which in turn is part of East Bay Regional Park District. Miller-Knox also includes undeveloped parkland with hiking trails in the hills and the nearby public Kellers Beach.

You'll have a great view of San Francisco Bay while you skate. Dornan Drive runs past the lake and picnic area, so you will hear some traffic noise during commute hours. A series of parking lots along Dornan provides plenty of free parking.

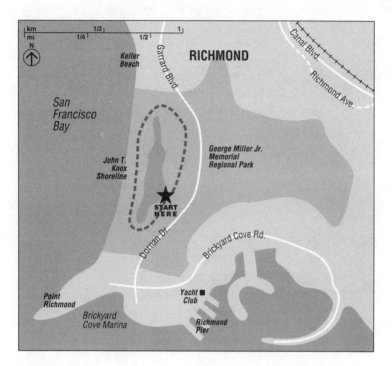

Most of the time this trail and the surrounding park are uncrowded, but on a few holidays (such as Easter Sunday and July Fourth), if the weather is good, it gets a little tight. Hardly any bicyclists use this path.

How to Get There by Car

From westbound Interstate 580, take the Castro Street/Point Richmond exit. Turn left at the light at the bottom of the off-ramp. Drive under the freeway, turn left on Tewksbury, and drive eastward. Turn right on Washington Street. You have just arrived in downtown Point Richmond. The last stop for food and water is the Santa Fe Market at the corner of Washington and Richmond Avenue. The market has an abundant variety of groceries but no prepared foods.

Turn left onto Richmond Avenue from Washington Street, and continue eastward for two extremely long blocks. *After* you cross a railroad track, which enters a railroad tunnel, you will see an automobile tunnel on your right on Garrard Boulevard. Turn right onto Garrard, switch on your headlights, go through the tunnel, and you will emerge on Dornan Drive (Garrard turns into Dornan). Follow Dornan Drive around the bend until you see parking lots on your right. Park anywhere. Turn off your headlights and look toward the bay.

What It's Like

The path is all asphalt in good condition. There is a little rough patch next to the parking lots at the north end of the park, but it shouldn't slow you down too much. At both the north and south ends of the pond you can choose longer or shorter routes.

On the west side of the pond, around the middle in the north-to-south direction, and just a few yards from the trail, you will see a concrete pad in excellent condition, several thousand square feet in area. The East Bay Regional Park workers keep this area swept and hazard-free as a picnic area for those in wheelchairs. Feel free to use it (when the physically disabled aren't wheeling about) for figure skating or roller hockey, or just for the thrill of rink-type skating without the confines or price of a rink.

There is a pickup hockey game most Sundays around 2 P.M. (Saturdays around 10 A.M. for kids), so along with your skates and wristguards, be sure to bring knee pads, elbow pads, and a helmet. And a hockey stick, just so you don't look out of place.

If you want to do some street skating, the town of Point Richmond lies just around the bend and through the tunnel from the park. Point Richmond is small enough that you can skate more or less safely down the middle of the street in the middle of the day; it's big enough, though, that you can get yourself a cappuccino at three different establishments. If you don't draw too much attention to yourself, you can get your cappuccino and drink it outside without even taking your skates off.

Places to Eat

If you want to skate to a meal, you can choose either of two directions.

You can skate south on Dornan Drive then follow the bends in the road as it turns left and becomes Brickyard Cove Road. Skate past the Richmond Yacht Club. Turn right into the driveway of Brickyard Cove Marina. At the far end of the parking lot, upstairs, is All's Fare (breakfast and lunch, open 7 A.M., closed Mon.). Great view, great food.

Or you can skate north from the park on Dornan Drive, retracing your steps through the tunnel. Be careful going in and out of the tunnel; this isn't recommended for beginners. Turn left at the corner of West Richmond Avenue, then right on Park Place (between the firehouse and the Point Orient Restaurant). Cruising down Park Place you can get something quick to eat at Rosemary's Bakery (opens at 6 A.M. Mon.–Sat.), Little Louie's (opens at 8 A.M.), or Edibles (opens at 7 A.M. Mon.–Sat.). All three serve skaters.

On your way back to the park, investigate Kellers Beach to the right of the tunnel. It's pretty steep, but you can skate right up to it.

Public Transportation

Miller-Knox Regional Park is readily accessible from San Francisco or the East Bay on the 73 bus line of AC Transit. You can get there from Marin County on the Golden Gate Transit line 40. Both of these bus lines run daily and connect with BART.

Other Trails to Check Out in the Neighborhood

Point Pinole

Chapter 10

Nimitz Way in Tilden Park

Ratings

Overall Rating	●●●
Path Surface	●●●
Public Transit Access	None
Surroundings	●●●●●
Level of Difficulty	Challenging
Length	4 miles one way

As you skate around the bay on the paths in this book, you may notice that some paths have four-by-four wooden signposts carved with "Bayview Trail," holding little metal leaf icons. These signs refer to the path-forming rapture that's coming when someday—maybe in the not-too-distant future—San Francisco Bay will be ringed by one continuous roller-skating path. It will no doubt be possible to circle the bay on this path just by following the little leaf icons—a veritable Macintosh of a skating trail. A few of the four-by-four signposts, though, are already missing their metal emblems, which in some cases makes them uninterpretable. Either the project took too long, or the signs just didn't last long enough. (If it were up to me, I would have carved all those little icons onto big rocks. It would probably have cost the same amount of money, too.)

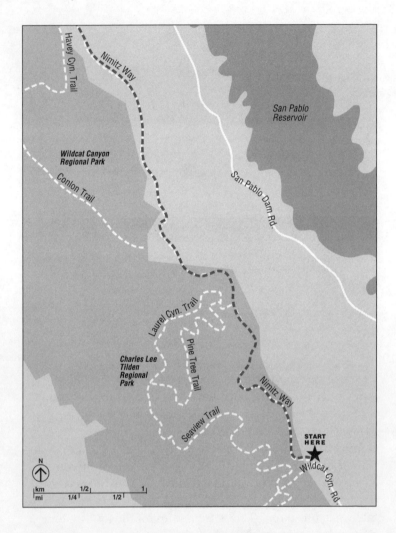

In the future, there is going to be another trail, called the Ridge Trail, circling the bay on the hilltops. Nimitz Way, in the hills above Kensington and El Cerrito and Orinda, is going to be part of that system.

Nimitz Way is a difficult trail, partly because of the cattle-crossing grates, but mostly because of the grades. Don't attempt it unless you stop at the store first and get new brake shoes. If you are still on your first set of brake shoes, don't go at all. One day, you'll know that you need new brakes, and you can let it remind you that it's time to go skating on Inspiration Point.

How to Get There by Car

From eastbound and westbound Interstate 80, take the University Avenue exit in Berkeley and stay in the left-hand lanes going east on University Avenue. At the very end of University, at the T-shaped intersection with Oxford Street, make a left into the far right lane of Oxford, then go one block and turn right onto Hearst Avenue. Go east on Hearst to a stoplight at the top of a hill, and turn right onto Gayley Road. Just before you get to the Cal Bears Memorial Stadium on your left, take the first left onto the rimway circling the stadium, and then make the next left onto North Canyon Road. North Canyon Road winds around by one of the university's swimming pools and the University Botanical Garden, then it becomes Centennial Drive. Up, up, up you drive on Centennial to Grizzly Peak Boulevard. Turn right on Grizzly Peak and follow the winding road a bit, keeping an eye out for South Park Drive. Turn left into Tilden Park on South Park Drive. (This street is closed certain months to allow the newts to cross the road during mating season.) Follow South Park to Wildcat Canyon Road. Take a right. It is 1.1 miles from the intersection of South Park Drive and Wildcat Canyon Road to Inspiration Point; when you see the Lakeview sign, Inspiration Point is 0.4 miles ahead, on your left.

Parking is usually a problem in the afternoons, approaching sundown.

What It's Like

If you parked by the stone entrance to the trail, take a second to walk over to the other side of the lot and gaze at Orinda.

Start skating through the turnstile arrangement by the road. After shouldering your way past the pedestrians, you find out right away whether you can negotiate this trail, because there is a steep downhill stretch near the beginning. If you make it to the bottom, fine. The trail is pretty close to the Hayward Fault, so you will be able to see some of those geological cracks so common hereabouts. (The Cal Bears football stadium has concrete that is displaced six inches vertically along the Hayward Fault.) Try out the benches placed here for admiring the view. You go through a woodsy part of the trail, very pleasant, then at approximately the 1.75-mile mark you come to the first cattle crossing. For all you newcomers to the West, these aren't crosswalks for cattle; these are heavy metal grates that will grab a cow's hoof (or your skate) and wrestle it to the ground. The idea is to go through the swing gate on the right. You have to stop and release the gate, go through it, then close it again. This isn't fun to do. There are a total of four of these grates and gates in the first three and a half miles of this four-mile trail. That's the bad news.

The good news is the scenery is fantastic. The views are panoramic. The pavement isn't too bad, and if you can keep up your momentum on the downslopes, the uphills are merely a good aerobic workout. Once you get past that second cattle crossing, you won't meet very many pedestrians. You and the bicyclists will have the trail to yourselves, and it is indeed a peaceful, quiet, and beautiful place.

The trail ends abruptly in a pile of dirt heaped unceremoniously at about the four-mile mark. When you get to the end, pause for a moment, look around you, and see if you can conjure up a Nike missile base. After Pearl Harbor, hilltops like this one were requisitioned for warfare. Look around, and imagine a ticky-tacky little town with little boxes on the hillsides.

The company town you are standing in was in the business of war. Offices hummed twenty-four hours a day, filling out forms, shipping and receiving, telephoning. Their mission was to be ready to launch nuclear warheads from those concrete pads to your right and up on the rise. When this place was really active, cresting the wave of paranoia that deposited it here forty years ago, those concrete pads were as smooth and hard and flat as a billiard table. Only the Defense Department had concrete like that. And look at it now. It's cracked and uprooted, and the aggregate is poking out of the concrete. Look at the wooden post, a weathered, barn-red four-by-four with a board attached to it crosswise, like a sign perhaps, or a place for posting a notice. Maybe it's all that's left of a sign that warned of the danger of radioactivity on the premises (they warehoused plutonium here, and it's hot for a hundred thousand years). What kind of sign were they going to hang on it to tell people to stay away—a sign that would last twenty times longer than recorded civilization? What sort of signpost were they going to nail that sign to? That four-by-four is already all that's left.

Skate back the way you skated in, on Nimitz Way. It's the road they built to service the missiles.

Places to Eat

Tilden Park doesn't offer much in the way of food. Maybe out here in the woods and fields one can imagine foraging for roots and berries as a hunter/gatherer, but such thoughts are dispelled whenever one of the steers wanders by or when you notice that not much native vegetation is left. You might want to grab something to eat on the way here, in Berkeley's Northside area. On Hearst, just after crossing Euclid Avenue, try the 3 C's Cafe. Parking is a problem. If you are looking for only a snack, you will find a hot dog stand in Tilden Park at the merry-go-round just off Wildcat Canyon Road. Go straight on Wildcat Canyon Road past South Park Drive, and follow the signs to Anza Lake and the merry-go-round—a magnificent old carousel.

Public Transportation

None.

Other Trails to Check Out in the Neighborhood

Berkeley's North Waterfront Park
BART from Berkeley to Richmond

Chapter 11

The Contra Costa Canal

Ratings

Overall Rating	●●
Path Surface	●●●
Public Transit Access	Almost ●●●●●
Surroundings	●
Level of Difficulty	Easy
Length	12 miles

As you drive around the Golden State of California, every once in a while you come across a long straight ribbon of water flowing determinedly from point A to point B, sometimes uphill. The general idea of this powered water movement is to draw water from the Sacramento River. On a federal level, the process is called reclamation. Way back before the Great War, the Bureau of Reclamation built the first leg of this canal here in Contra Costa County, California, to reclaim the dry countryside and turn it into farms.

The canal was finished sometime in the fifties. Contra Costa County has grown up around the canal, following the curves of the waterway with clusters of cul-de-sacs. The canal is a truncated loop, a U-shaped concrete ditch, with water flowing downhill from the hills above Concord, swooping around through Walnut Creek, and going back the way it came into Martinez. Surprisingly long portions of this loop are uninterrupted by road crossings.

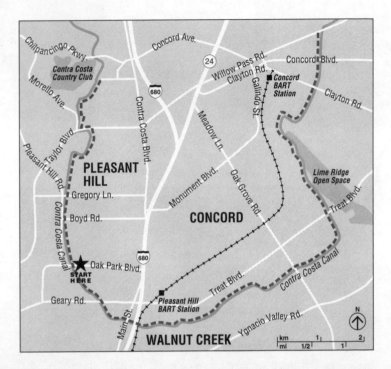

The pumps are now staffed by the Contra Costa Water District. The skating path along the waterway is officially an East Bay Regional Park District Regional Trail; it doubles as an access road for the water district's pickup trucks, mostly at night. When the water district needs to work on part of the canal, a section of trail gets fenced off.

How to Get There by Car

From Interstate 680 north, exit at Treat Boulevard/Geary Road in Walnut Creek, and take a left at the bottom of the off-ramp to go west on Geary Road. Go about a mile on Geary, and turn right on Pleasant Hill Road. A half mile later, Pleasant Hill Road curves right, then at an odd sort of intersection where Pleasant Hill Road veers left again, you continue straight onto Oak Park Boulevard. The trail crosses Oak Park Boulevard just after the capacious parking lots of the Onstage Theater.

From Interstate 680 south, take the Main Street/Geary Road exit and turn left onto Main Street in Walnut Creek. A block later, turn right onto Geary Road. Go right on Pleasant Hill Road, follow it around the bend a mile later, then go straight on Oak Park Boulevard when Pleasant Hill Road veers left again. Park anywhere. The trail crosses Oak Park Boulevard just east of Oak Creek Court.

To start skating at the middle of the trail, exit Interstate 680 at Geary Road/Treat Boulevard and take Treat Boulevard east. Turn right on Oak Grove Road (no relation) and stop at Graymont. The trail crosses Oak Grove Road between Graymont and Peachwillow Lane.

To start at the other end of the trail, take Interstate 680 to Willow Pass Road exit in Concord, and go east on Willow Pass. Turn right on Sixth Street, then left on The Alameda. At the bend in the road, park anywhere. You can't miss it.

What It's Like

If you parked near Oak Park Boulevard in Pleasant Hill and started skating north, the skating trail is intersected by very few streets. Of the few streets that do cross it, both Boyd Road and Gregory Lane require patience. At Taylor Boulevard you have to take a detour to the crosswalk. At Las Juntas Park the path becomes so steep that beginners might consider turning around. The section between Taylor and Chilpancingo Parkway is beautiful—it rolls up and down by the end of the Contra Costa Country Club and by Diablo Valley College's Center for the Performing Arts.

If you started this trail in the middle, where the canal crosses Oak Grove Road, go west from Oak Grove Road and have a relaxing roll toward Bancroft Avenue and beyond. It is astonishing that so much quiet, open space exists in the middle of such a built-up area.

At the upriver section of the canal, the landscape seems even more rural. If you skate far enough south from Clayton Road you will be running along the border of Lime Ridge Open Space, a grassland that the voters decided should always stay just about the way it is now.

Places to Eat

The Contra Costa Canal Trail crosses Bancroft Avenue just a few hundred feet south of the corner of the Bancroft Shopping Center. The Copper Kettle Restaurant has an outdoor seating area, suitable for feeding a group of hungry skaters. Open early and late.

Public Transportation

The trail is a block or two south of the Pleasant Hill BART station on Oak Road.

Other Trails to Check Out in the Neighborhood

The Iron Horse Trail from Walnut Creek to San Ramon. Someday the Iron Horse Trail will intersect the Contra Costa Canal Trail, just three blocks south of the Pleasant Hill BART station.

Ygnacio Canal Trail. Ygnacio Valley Road crosses Oak Grove Road three blocks south of the Contra Costa Canal Trail. From the intersection of Ygnacio Valley and Oak Grove, head east on Ygnacio Valley; where the road curves left and starts to climb into the hills, look for a parking/staging area on the right. It isn't marked. The Ygnacio Canal Trail is hiding to the right of the highway. Skate east on that trail, and see some dazzling overlooks from high above the treetops of Concord. The trail leads through a custom-built tunnel under Ygnacio Valley Road. When you reach a T-intersection and a 5 m.p.h. sign, you might want to stop and turn back, because it is indeed steep. If you do skate down it, the path merges with a newly paved portion of the Contra Costa Canal Trail.

Chapter 12

The Lafayette-Moraga Regional Trail

Ratings

Overall Rating	●●
Path Surface	●● (longitudinal cracks)
Public Transit Access	●●●●
Surroundings	● (cross traffic)
Level of Difficulty	Medium
Length	About 4 miles one way

The Lafayette-Moraga Regional Trail is built on the roadbed of the former Sacramento Northern Railroad. The zigs and zags and sharp ups and downs in the first part of the trail mostly result from the ripping out of bridges. Therefore, we will not start this trail at the Park District's official staging area but at a place a mile up the path.

The East Bay Regional Park District keeps this trail up. We don't think about it much, but the EBRPD is a remarkable organization. The park district has had integrated work crews for decades now, free (at least it appears so to outsiders) of racism and sexism. Park district police take a hard line on drugs, drinking, and gang activity in the parks. Workers have consensus meetings to make sure that everybody's concerns

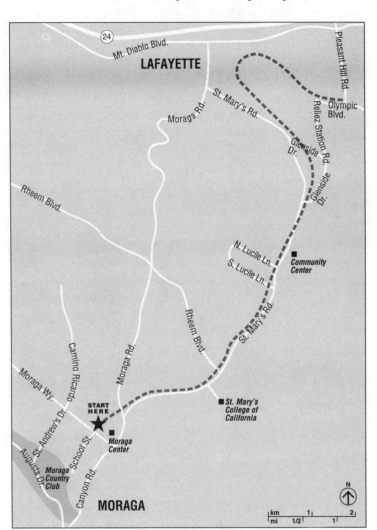

are being heard and that everybody is pulling in the same direction. A remarkable organization indeed. It is a testament to the organization's right thinking that as long-and-skinny rights-of-way like this one have become available, the EBRPD has chosen to take them under its wing. They treat unconventional spaces like these trails with the same respect for nature they have for their more conventional park spaces featuring the usual groves of trees and babbling brooks.

How to Get There by Car

From Highway 24, eastbound or westbound, take the Orinda/Moraga exit.

From the eastbound side (those of you who just came out of the Caldecott Tunnel), make a right at the bottom of the off-ramp, following the signs for Moraga. For a very short stretch you will be on Camino Pablo, then you bear right onto Moraga Way. Don't bear too far right, though, or you will end up on Camino Encinas. Moraga Way is the one that looks more like a highway.

From the westbound side (those of you coming from Walnut Creek or Sacramento or New York City via Interstate 680), make a left at the bottom of the off-ramp, following the signs for Orinda/Moraga; do not head right to Orinda Village. You are now heading south on Camino Pablo; if you stay in the middle lane past the stoplight after the freeway underpass, you will be heading south on Moraga Way.

Once on Moraga Way, head south about four miles. It's very pleasant, bucolic, and ritzy. After you pass St. Andrew's Drive on your right and then a firehouse, slow down and look for a shopping center on your right. The street that forms the left side of the parking lot of the shopping center and is essentially incorporated into the shopping center is School Street. Make a left onto School Street, and drive to the end. You're there. Trust me.

What It's Like

For us, the trail starts at Moraga Ranch, a collection of old red wooden buildings on the west side of School Street in the town of Moraga. On the right is a shopping center, with a Safeway and a Macalou's (a very popular store in these parts). This center is the only place to buy a snack along this trail. Put on your skates and head northeast on the wide concrete trail.

As you go through an old orchard, the concrete is soon superseded by asphalt. From here on, you are forced to take notice of California's geological instability: there are longitudinal cracks in the asphalt along almost the entire length of this trail. In at least one instance, one side of the crack has subsided over three inches from the other side. In California, you don't close trails merely because they're a little geologically unstable. Just be careful that one of those fissures doesn't reach up and grab one of your blades and wrestle you abruptly to the ground.

The trail crosses Moraga Road (not Moraga Way) and continues on through Moraga Commons. It makes an abrupt left and then a right going through the commons; avoid the playground, and try to find the East Bay Regional Park District bulletin board. Pick up a copy of the EBRPD trail map. You will be skating parallel to St. Mary's Road, following a par course, and going decidedly uphill.

The trail is clearly marked with distances from either end. About one mile from Moraga Ranch, you will see St. Mary's College on your right, across the road. Just a few hundred feet more, and you will find a lovely picnic area, just before you get to Rheem Boulevard. It's very scenic and usually deserted—a good place to eat the lunch stuff you bought at the Safeway.

If you turn back here, you'll avoid the traffic farther on and keep the prevailing wind at your back. If you continue, after you cross Rheem Boulevard the trail goes decidedly downhill—both literally and figuratively. The longitudinal cracks are much in evidence here. A one-mile stretch is uninterrupted by automobile cross traffic until you get to South Lucile Lane, just inside the Lafayette city limits. Families with young children should definitely turn around here.

After this point, you do a lot of starting and stopping at intersections. The most serious of these is at St. Mary's Road, just after the Lafayette Community Center. Beware of the fast-moving automobiles.

The rest of the trail is like a little whistle-stop tour of the backyards of Lafayette. You end up actually skating in the street at Brookdale Court. One mile from the end of the trail, there is no path per se, and you are skating through the yard of the Moraga Pumping Plant of the East Bay Municipal Utility District. Forewarned is forearmed; have faith, and you will emerge at the other end of the pumping plant glad that you bought this book.

The trail ends at the Olympic Boulevard Staging Area, the official name for the two parking lots at the corner of Olympic Boulevard and Pleasant Hill Road. (The trail appears to continue after the first little parking lot, but it only takes you to the second parking lot.)

On your second trip to this trail, you might want to get off Highway 24 at the Pleasant Hill Road exit and start skating from this end of the trail, heading back to Moraga Ranch. To do that, go south on Pleasant Hill Road and right on Olympic Boulevard to Reliez Station Road.

Places to Eat

Stop in at the Cookhouse Cafe (510-376-3477) at Moraga Ranch at the very beginning of this trail. Skaters are welcome! However, this charming little establishment has a lovely waxed wooden floor. It's so polished, you could dance on it or eat off it, but it's a real challenge to skate on it. Sunday hours are limited to 9 A.M. to 12 P.M., which is just right for skaters.

Public Transportation

The easiest way to get to the Lafayette-Moraga Regional Trail is from the Lafayette BART station. Take the County Connection 123 bus line to St. Mary's College and start skating in the middle of the trail.

Telephone 510-676-7500 for County Connection information.

You can also take the 106 line from BART to Moraga.

Other Trails to Check Out in the Neighborhood

The Contra Costa Canal

Chapter 13

The Iron Horse Trail from Walnut Creek to San Ramon

Ratings	
Overall Rating	●●●●
Path Surface	●●●; some ●●●●
Public Transit Access	●●●●
Surroundings	●●
Level of Difficulty	Easy
Length	15 miles

As of 1994, the Iron Horse Trail has twelve miles of contiguous skating path, running from Rudgear Road in Walnut Creek to Pine Valley Road in San Ramon. It was nicknamed the Iron Horse when it was part of the Southern Pacific railroad line. Someday it will be over thirty miles long, according to the blurbs of the East Bay Regional Park District.

Start in the middle of the trail in downtown Danville. The path south of Danville to San Ramon is a straightaway through a soon-to-be-developed industrial park, and the southernmost portion is especially suited for beginners and kids. The path north, toward Walnut Creek, goes past horse farms. In the middle, in Danville, the trail has a discontinuity that has been only partially clarified by the street signs. That's

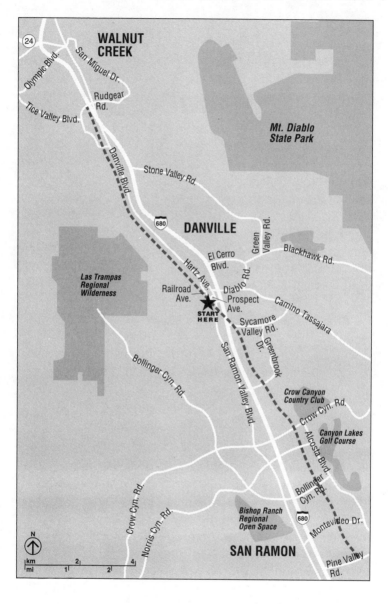

why I think it's best to start after having a cup of coffee and a snack at the genuine French bakery on Railroad Avenue.

Before you try this trail for the first time, call the National Park Service for a reservation for Eugene O'Neill's place. O'Neill is still the only American dramatist to win a Nobel prize. His wife Carlotta moved him to Danville in the forties to get him away from distractions. (That was before the freeway was constructed.) The house they built with the prize money is actually in Las Trampas Wilderness, just outside Danville on Kuss Road. If O'Neill were around, he would no doubt want to inspect his house now that it's a National Historic Landmark. I suspect that he would take a trip out to see it and then write about it the same way he wrote about those other unlikely places—freighters, barges, cheap hotels, seedy bars. And he wouldn't fail to notice that not a single scrap of paper with his work on it can be found anywhere around the place.

After you get back from O'Neill's, check out the Farmer's Market in the same parking lot where the park service picks you up and drops you off. O'Neill would have done that, just to watch the people and listen to them talk. Authentic dialogue. He practically invented it.

How to Get There by Car

From southbound or northbound Interstate 680, take the Diablo Road exit in Danville. Head west on Diablo Road into town until you get to the main drag, Hartz Avenue. (Note that you have to drive through the base of a clock tower to do this.) Try to park anywhere on or around the next street over, Railroad Avenue. Here, the Iron Horse Trail runs behind Railroad Avenue and the shopping mall mentioned earlier. You can cross the trail by turning left onto Hartz from Diablo Road, then right on Prospect.

What It's Like

I recommend that you begin with the southern part of this trail. First fortify yourself with something from Pascal's bakery and then head down the sidewalk in front of the mini-mall to Prospect Avenue. You will see the trail going off to the right. Instead, look for the black-and-white street sign saying Iron Horse Trail; it resembles a one-way sign. This sign points you left down Railroad Avenue. You skate briefly in the street, jog left on Church Street, and skate through a parking lot (where the Farmer's Market is held). Continue to follow the black-and-white street signs. At San Ramon Valley Boulevard, the trail takes you across the intersection of San Ramon Valley Boulevard and Interstate 680. The marking system seems to break down, though, where the trail crosses Sycamore Valley Road.

From this point on and south, the Iron Horse Trail consists of long, straight, uneventful stretches of asphalt. The pavement is in bad shape near Crow Canyon Road, but only at the intersection itself. At Norris Canyon Road is a patch of truly excellent blacktop followed by concrete with wide expansion joints as you approach Bollinger Canyon Road. Look over to the left on Bollinger Canyon Road. You can skate in that direction to the community center, where you will find some very nice pavement for figure skating; or cross the street to get to the skate shop in the Market Place mall, in the back of the Any Mountain store.

The last mile and a half of the trail is truly uneventful. If you like wide open spaces, this is it. Good pavement, too. The Iron Horse Trail now ends abruptly at Pine Valley Road, though it may be extended in the future.

From downtown Danville to Pine Valley and back is well over ten miles.

If you want to skate some more, go north on the trail you spotted off to the right of our starting point at Pascal's in

Danville. You'll pass through remarkable rural landscapes. Around Livorna Road are some beautiful horse ranches. This trail is harder on children and beginners, though. It's a five-mile whistle-stop tour through backyards and street crossings. But for the last two and a half miles before the staging area at Rudgear Road (the confluence of Walnut Creek's Main Street, Danville Boulevard, and Interstate 680), you have to cross only five streets.

Places to Eat

When you get to the southern end of the trail, you might want to go a little way east on Bollinger Canyon Road to the Market Place. In the middle of the mall is Espresso Romano (510-867-1100), open for coffee, drinks, and pastry at 7 A.M. (On Sundays, this is all they serve; other days they serve sandwiches, too.)

If you get to Danville while they're holding the Farmer's Market, help yourself to some of the finest fruits, vegetables, smoked fish, bread, and preserves to be found on a roller-skating trail anywhere. If you want some genuine French pastry, roll on in to Gilbert Sonet's Pascal French Oven at 125 Railroad Avenue (510-838-7349; open Mon.–Sat. 6 A.M. to 5 P.M., Sun. 7:30 A.M. to 3:00 P.M.). If you want a sit-down meal, roll into the Uptown Cafe (510-838-8588), located across Hartz Avenue from Pascal's, and sit yourself down outdoors. Skates and kids okay. Superb.

Places to Rent Skates

Try Any Mountain (510-275-1010) at the Market Place, across the parking lot from Romano's side door. Just don't try to answer any of the Any Mountain rental person's questions, like, "Do you want ABEC precision bearings or . . . ?" If you do, you will get out of there in about twenty-five minutes. If you simply say, "Anything that rolls," you'll be out in five.

Public Transportation

The County Connection 121 line can get you to the Iron Horse Trail from Walnut Creek BART.

Other Trails to Check Out in the Neighborhood

The Contra Costa Canal
The Lafayette-Moraga Regional Trail

Chapter 14

BART *from Berkeley to Richmond*

Ratings	
Overall Rating	●
Path Surface	Mostly ●●●●; some ●●●●●
Public Transit Access	●●●●●
Surroundings	●
Level of Difficulty	Easy
Length	About 4 miles one way

Transportation evolves. What was once an efficient mode of movement becomes, for one reason or another, not so efficient.

That's what happened to the Atchison Topeka and Santa Fe Railroad, which ran a team track through here when people still used teams of horses to deliver freight. Now the freight-handling capabilities of that train have been elegantly supplanted by the marvels of intermodalism. The passenger stations in Berkeley have been turned into restaurants and bars (like the Sante Fe Bar & Grill on University Avenue). And the tracks have been turned into roller-skating trails.

The one thing you won't see on this trail is vestigial rails, as you can observe in Monterey or Sausalito. The Santa Fe had replaced its rickety old jointed track with brand-new 119-pound

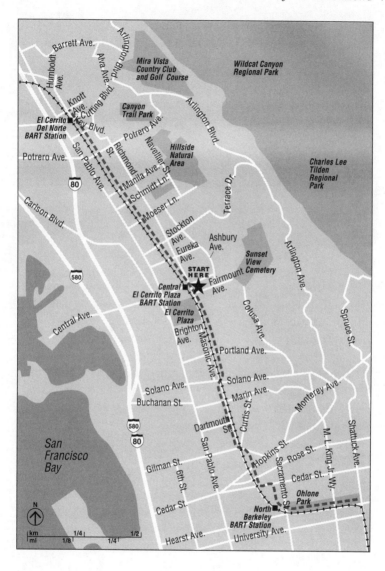

rail just prior to selling the route to BART, and they ripped this rail up and reused it somewhere else in the Santa Fe system. Slick.

How to Get There by Car

From northbound or southbound Interstates 80 or 580, take the Central Avenue exit and head east on Central. Go about a mile, turn right on Richmond Street, cross Fairmount Avenue, and park in the staging area where Richmond Street dead-ends.

What It's Like

It's, like, urban.

But that having been said, the strip of asphalt beneath and slightly to the side of the elevated BART tracks is just far enough off the beaten path to be a good place to skate. Like the railroad it replaced, the path goes through backyards and alleys and crosses at least one major thoroughfare.

From the staging area, start skating north past the City of El Cerrito/Ohlone Greenway/At Fairmount Avenue sign. That's the El Cerrito Plaza BART station up above. The Greenway refers to the landscaping done by the City of El Cerrito, with a par course featuring a questionably useful jumping-jack pad as well as other *useful* items like a chin-up bar. There is a playground for the kids at Fairmount Avenue. This is good smooth asphalt, maybe worth a five-star rating. The Greenway groundskeepers have planted lots of young trees, and a bit of mulch and twigs can be found on the trail at times, but it's not too bad. Each section of the trail is a block long at this point, except at Eureka Avenue, where there is a ramp up to the street on the right. At Schmidt Lane, the kids will be delighted that "You Are Now Entering the Dinosaur Forest." The Department of Motor Vehicles has a parking lot at Manila

Avenue that is unused on weekends, definitely a five-star surface; similarly, the basketball court between Manila Street and Potrero Avenue is good for a little figure skating. When you get to Cutting Boulevard, you have gone one complete BART stop to the El Cerrito del Norte station. You have to jog left at Cutting, then at Knott Avenue you skate through a parking lot. This parking lot detour is all part of the officially marked and sanctioned trail; it lends a whole new meaning to the word *variance*. The trail ends abruptly at Key, at the End of Bike Path sign.

If you bear left on Humboldt Avenue (a little street skating here), you will see an amazing rock in the front yard of number 2218. Definitely something you don't see every day. You can grab some refreshment at the Del Norte Place on Wall Avenue, near the end of the trail.

Back at the staging area beneath El Cerrito BART, if you decide to skate more, head south on the same trail, past El Cerrito Plaza on your right. It's another whistle-stop tour with lots of cross streets. After you cross busy Solano Avenue, you'll find quite a bit of open space. It's downright parklike after Marin Avenue, paralleling Masonic Avenue. After you cross Dartmouth and are approaching the three-corner intersection with Gilman Street, stay to the left. The most recent section of the trail is on the other side of Gilman.

The southern section of this trail doesn't die, nor does it fade away. With a great deal of perseverance, you can hack your way past some tennis courts at Hopkins Street, around Cedar-Rose Park, past a basketball court, and around the North Berkeley BART station. On the other side of the BART station (BART is underground by this point) the City of Berkeley has constructed Ohlone Park, which has wide concrete trails suitable for skating, all the way up to Shattuck Avenue.

The section of trail from Fairmount Avenue in El Cerrito to Gilman Street in Berkeley (the recommended excursion here) is just over two miles one way.

Places to Eat

At the north end of the trail are some delightful places to sit outside and enjoy a bite to eat. As you head south from the end of the trail at Key, turn off the path at Wall Avenue, and skate into Del Norte Place. At JR Muggs (open at 6 A.M.! weekdays) it's okay to skate in and order a cappuccino and snacks. Later in the day and into the evening, you can find more elegant fare at String's Italian Cafe. Skate right up.

At the south end of the trail is an outdoor dining area managed by Brothers Bagels and Toot Sweets. It's at the Gilman Street crossing. Brothers Bagels is a few yards away on Gilman.

Public Transportation

The Del Norte and El Cerrito BART stations perch above the trail.

Other Trails to Check Out in the Neighborhood

Berkeley's North Waterfront Park
Nimitz Way in Tilden Park

Chapter 15

Berkeley's North Waterfront Park

Ratings	
Overall Rating	●●
Path Surface	●●; ●●●●● (waterfront loop)
Public Transit Access	●●●●
Surroundings	●●; ●●●●● (waterfront loop)
Level of Difficulty	Easy
Length	1 mile for the waterfront loop only

The City of Berkeley brought in truckload after truckload of trash and garbage and mixed it proportionately with dirt and concrete to create Berkeley Marina's North Waterfront Park. There were a few problems, of course, like the road that wouldn't stay flat (the locals used to come out and watch cars galumphing down that road, and they'd cheer at each especially powerful case of constructive interference). But in general, this custom-made little land mass came out pretty much like the real thing.

What we have is rather like the Miller-Knox Regional Park path in Point Richmond, which, come to think of it, is also synthetic. You'll find a pleasant, circular skating path in a park, great for kids and beginners, connected to a coffee shop by a trail that's a bit more challenging and so doesn't get a lot of traffic.

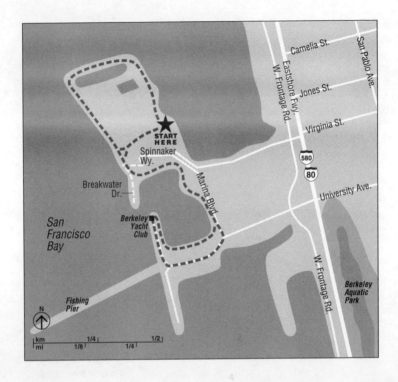

How to Get There by Car

From westbound Interstate 80, take the Gilman Street exit. At the bottom of the off-ramp, jog to the right as you cross the street, and continue south on Frontage Road, which parallels the freeway. When you get to the next stop sign at University Avenue, take a right (that's the Seabreeze Market opposite). Drive one extremely long block to Marina Boulevard, and turn right at the sign that says North Waterfront Park. After another long block, the road curves to the left and becomes Spinnaker Way. Try to grab a parking space near the curve. The trail is on the other side of the trees.

From eastbound Interstate 80, exit at Powell Street in Emeryville. Stay in the second lane from the left, and turn left onto Powell Street at the bottom of the off-ramp. Shift to the far right lane, and turn right onto Frontage Road just before the Shell station. After a few miles, you will see the Seabreeze Market on your left at the intersection with University Avenue. Take a left onto University, make a right on Marina, go right at the sign that says North Waterfront Park, and park after you go past the Marriott.

When you're ready to go home, you can get back to 80 eastbound (Albany, Sacramento, or New York) or 580 westbound (Richmond or Marin) by going north on Frontage Road at the Seabreeze, turning right at the racetrack, passing under the freeway, and turning left up the ramp.

To get back to 80 westbound or 580 eastbound (San Jose, Oakland, San Francisco), just hop on the freeway on-ramp across the street from the Seabreeze. It's a quick left.

What It's Like

If you were able to get a parking space by the bend in the road where Marina Boulevard turns into Spinnaker Way, look around for the three-foot-tall map cast in concrete. It's a nice touch and will no doubt outlast most of what it depicts. From here, start skating north along the bay. It's excellent pavement in spots, with nicely engineered gentle curves. There are even a few gentle swales built into the land. By the time you have made it around another curve and are heading west, you notice that this is relatively hassle-free skating. When you make the turn onto the continuation of Breakwater Drive, you are skating along the bay, looking straight out at the Golden Gate. They could have called the park New Oceanview, after the old Oceanview neighborhood of Berkeley, whose view is blocked by the new land mass.

When you get to the traffic circle at the end of Spinnaker Way, where all the kites are flying, you might want to turn left and rink around the track. It's a popular place among the locals.

If you are feeling adventurous, go straight at the traffic circle along Breakwater Drive and head toward the skyscrapers of Oakland and Emeryville. When you see the boat-launching ramps, veer left along the harbor. Go past the big parking lots on the left and two Marriott buildings, then bear right to Hornblower's dock. This is a public shore, open to all.

That glass hexagonal building just off the trail houses the Marriott's swimming pool. Outside the pool and before you get to the jazz lounge you will find a patio, where in good weather anyone can roll in, take a seat, and order a drink.

The trail around the Marriott going toward Marina Boulevard is under attack both from erupting tree roots and by subsidence of the landfill. Exercise caution. Go right on the sidewalk that parallels Marina Boulevard for a short distance, then head right on University Avenue; take the lower sidewalk, the one through the grove of redwoods. The concrete pad in front of you is a ferry dock; it last saw action after the '89 quake. The surface is only two stars; skip it. Continue along the marina, and soon you come to a little plaza with some good pavement and a very professional piece of monumental, abstract minimalist art (by Joe Slusky) to figure-skate around. Take note, all you amateur semioticians out there, that this is the only sculpture I have ever seen accompanied by a sign announcing that it is a sculpture.

Just around the corner from Mr. Slusky's sculpture are a store, a telephone, and a bus stop.

Follow the asphalt trail that leads out toward the ocean, curving to the right past hundreds of expensive sailboats and over to the Berkeley Yacht Club. The pavement is showing its age here. When you get all the way out to the yacht club, turn around and skate south along the breakwater that leads to the restaurant. You probably think I'm making this up, but that restaurant is named Skates. Skates by the Bay, to be exact. But if you try to skate in from the bay and order a drink at Skates, you will be told (in another semiotic singularity) that "the name doesn't really mean anything" and they don't serve skaters. Just remember this spot and go back to Skates without your skates during the winter, when the Berkeley wind whipping up the salt spray provides a truly bone-chilling experience. That is when Skates's window seats are magical; you are floating above the water with lights twinkling out on the bay like stars in the firmament. The food's not bad either.

The trail gets a bit rough. On the right is the Berkeley fishing pier. It has many bad joints and is off-limits to skaters anyway.

Take a left here and head back toward town on the path to the left of University Avenue. Stop to admire *The Guardian,* Fred Fierstein's archery sculpture in the middle of the intersection. The arrow is aimed at Asia. This fifteen-foot enlargement of a seventh-century Chinese key chain ornament wasn't authorized by the city government; in fact, the city wanted to remove it. Fred put it on the ballot in 1986, and the voters kept it.

After you get back to the store and the Slusky sculpture (which was duly authorized by the city), retrace your path by the ferry dock, the Marriott, and the boat ramp, to the traffic circle at Spinnaker Way and Breakwater Drive. Go right, and return to the concrete map marker.

For lunch you can skate to the Seabreeze Market on a path that runs south along Marina Boulevard. Take a left at University, stay on the north side of the street for one long block, and you're there. Next time, you could park your car at the Seabreeze and skate over to North Waterfront Park for a few laps or a picnic.

Places to Eat

The Seabreeze Market has outdoor tables, a variety of fruits and vegetables, a coffee bar, and tasty prepared food. Check out the clam chowder in a hollowed-out sourdough roll.

For years a hot dog vendor has set up shop across from Fred's archery sculpture. The hot dogs are surprisingly good.

Places to Rent Skates

You can rent skates at Berkeley Windsurfing (510-527-9283) on San Pablo Avenue, a little south of the intersection of San Pablo and Gilman Street.

If you don't mind going a little out of your way, try Karim's (510-841-2181) at 2801 Telegraph Avenue. This is the premiere place to rent or buy your skates, especially if you're after in-lines. If you go in and say, "I just want to go down to the Marina and try it out," Adlai Karim will hand you a pair of skates and administer his Zen-like blessing: "Keep it simple." The skates will work just right.

Public Transportation

The Berkeley Marina is at the end of the line for AC Transit's 51M line from Berkeley BART. No other 51 will do. It's got to be a 51M.

The ferry doesn't stop here anymore.

Amtrak's Berkeley station is right across the overpass from the Seabreeze Market.

Other Trails to Check Out in the Neighborhood

BART from Berkeley to Richmond
Nimitz Way in Tilden Park

Chapter 16

Alameda's
Southshore Trail

Overall Rating	●●
Path Surface	●●●; some ●●
Public Transit Access	●●●
Surroundings	●●
Level of Difficulty	Easy
Length	About 2.5 miles one way

The island of Alameda is one of the few places around San Francisco Bay where you can actually go swimming. At Alameda's Southshore no riptides zip people unexpectedly out to sea, and on some days this shallow water is warm enough to splash around in for as long as you want. The first mile or so of this trail is perfect for beginners, and it's next to the beach and the bay. It's also next to the road, but there are no cross streets and you will get lots of fresh air.

How to Get There by Car

If you're going southbound on 880, take the High Street/Alameda exit. Stay on the right side of the off-ramp and follow the signs for Alameda. (The signs for Oakland also refer to High Street, but in the wrong direction; you want to head west.) Turn right on High Street at the Shell station at the bottom of the off-ramp.

If you're northbound on 880, take the High Street/Alameda exit and turn left at the bottom of the off-ramp. Go under the freeway, heading west on High Street.

Once on High Street, drive west over the drawbridge. Stay in the left lane. Immediately after crossing the bridge to the island, turn left on Fernside Boulevard. When you get to the light at Otis Drive, take a right, then take a left on Bayview Drive. Curve around on Bayview until it ends at Broadway. Park on Bayview if possible and go left on Broadway on skates.

What It's Like

Alameda's Southshore Trail begins at the curve where Broadway becomes Shore Line Drive. The first quarter mile of the trail has better pavement than the rest of it and is especially good for a family outing. Near the trailhead you will find bathrooms provided by the East Bay Regional Park District.

On your left is the Elsie Roemer Bird Sanctuary. If you don't see many shorebirds or migratory birds from the trail, follow the short pier that juts out into the bay a few dozen yards from the trailhead and look around. If you forgot anything from the house, you can pick it up at the South Shore Center shopping mall a little ways up Shore Line Drive on your right, just past the McDonald's.

After you pass the bird sanctuary, you'll see splendid views of the beach and San Francisco Bay. After you pass Sand Castle picnic area about a mile north on the trail, the pavement becomes pretty rough. The path curves away from the beach, out toward the parking lots, then heads back toward the beach, on either side of a long driveway leading to the snack bar. It doesn't matter which little strip of asphalt you pick paralleling the driveway; they're all rough. The trail continues north on the right side of the snack bar building, where it runs alongside Robert W. Crown Memorial State Beach's Crab Cove Visitor Center. The visitor center proper is on your right (open Wed.–Sun. 10 to 4:30). The Marine Preserve, on your left, is open twenty-four hours a day.

The path continues around a point jutting out into the bay, then passes through a gate onto private property. That gate will remain open until just past dark. The "public shore" pathway through this private land continues bumpily for about a quarter mile, past Queens Road and past Kings Road, then ends abruptly at Crown Drive (probably no relation).

Places to Eat

On the other side of Shore Line Drive from the trailhead, near the bird sanctuary, is a McDonald's, where skaters have always been tolerated.

At the other end of the trail, near Crown Beach, you can skate up McKay Avenue to Central Avenue, hang a right on Central, pass Webster Street, cross the street, and skate into the backyard of Croll's Pizza and Croll's Tavern. You can yell your order through the screen door, and they will bring your food out. Croll's has tons of character; it's been there for a hundred years. If you do go inside, you'll see interesting old photos, stained glass, and, best of all, a vintage pinball machine in fairly good working order (Hee Haw, for the cognoscenti).

Tucker's ice cream parlor on Park Street is worth going out of your way for on your ride home. Just drive a short distance north on Shore Line Drive, turn right on Park Street, and drive all the way across the island. When the Park Street Bridge is in sight, look on your right for the ice cream parlor.

Places to Rent Skates

At 1431 Park Street you will find a skate shop called Willows Skate and Surf (510-523-5566).

Public Transportation

You can get to Alameda on the AC Transit 51 bus line. The 51 runs all the way from Berkeley and can take you within a block or two of the trail at either the Broadway and San Jose Avenue end to the south, or the Central and Webster end to the north. The 51 bus stops at the 12th Street BART station.

Other Trails to Check Out in the Neighborhood

Bay Farm Island

Chapter 17

Bay Farm Island

Ratings

Overall Rating	●●●
Path Surface	●●●; some ●● and ●●●●●
Public Transit Access	●●●●
Surroundings	●●
Level of Difficulty	Easy
Length	A loop of about 6 miles

When you arrive at Bay Farm Island, you will probably find a few skaters tooling around by the industrial condos along Harbor Bay Parkway. Perhaps the businesslike appearance of the tiltups in the neighborhood inspires the determined, gymnastic, back-and-forth skatercising you often see down by South Loop Road and in the parking lot across from the ferry dock.

Take a brisk excursion all the way around the island, a loop that's excellent for beginners and virtuosos alike. You will see stunning views of San Francisco Bay half the way around, and cross traffic at only one point.

How to Get There by Car

Exit Interstate 880 at Hegenberger Road in Oakland. South-bound, it's Hegenberger Road *west*, the *first* right from the off-ramp. Northbound, you exit onto Edes Avenue, then take a

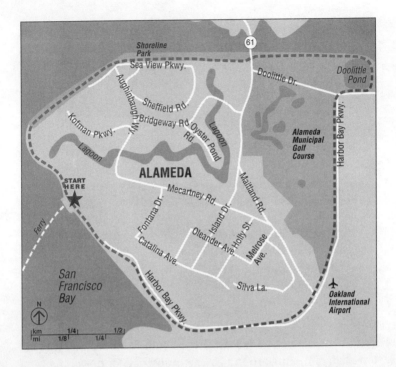

left onto Hegenberger. Follow all the signs for Oakland Airport.

Just after the Hilton Hotel on Hegenberger, take a right on Doolittle Drive. Follow Doolittle for a few miles (note the interesting park on your right and the very interesting North Field airport facilities on your left, including a museum), then take a left on an imposing boulevard called Harbor Bay Parkway and drive another few miles. The road seems to peter out, but have faith and motor on, first following the Ferry sign and later the Harbor Bay Maritime sign. Eventually you will arrive at a capacious parking lot. This is it.

On your next trip to Bay Farm Island, you might want to take that ferry ride. It's great. Goes right to Pier 39 in San Francisco, for example.

What It's Like

The path begins at the ferry dock, takes you northwest half a mile or so, then curves northeast for another mile through Shoreline Park. The path varies from excellent to old to wet; when the condo owners run their sprinklers early in the day, the pavement can get slippery, especially for in-lines. Just after the Bay Farm Island Recreation Center, you will see a drawbridge (which works). Skate under that bridge and continue on the other side. Here you'll find some great pavement, all the way around the bend to the Bill Osborne Model Airplane Field, where for ten dollars (skaters welcome) you and your family can fly a noisy, gas-powered model plane and emulate a takeoff from the aircraft carrier USS *Enterprise*. This little exercise takes on a whole new aura of verisimilitude when a single-engine airplane takes off at the same time from the adjoining North Field of Oakland International and wags its wings to you as it thunders mightily by.

Skate across Doolittle Drive at the crosswalk near the Oakland City Limit sign. Follow the Harbor Bay Business Park sign toward the Alameda Municipal Golf Course. The trail is the serviceable asphalt path along Harbor Bay Parkway that you saw from your car.

To your left, you'll see an aspect of aviation most of us never get to know. Instead of 747s and DC10s roosting by the passenger terminal, here you'll find several biplanes that belong to the Aerial Advertising Company; you wouldn't believe how they pick those banners up. You can also inspect some truly remarkable airplane wrecks. A sign lets you know that a bit farther down the path is a "teleport."

Somewhere along the Champs-Elysées–like Harbor Bay Parkway where South Loop Road turns into North Loop Road, this skating path crosses over into the surreal. It may not be the surreal of André Breton's manifesto or Salvador Dali's paintings, but it's close. Number 1201 Harbor Bay Parkway, for example, is the home of American President Systems, an ocean shipping company that has its entrance on a fountain with no water. In front of number 1220 is a huge sculpture fountain that manages to appear both spectacular and mundane. The water is dyed, you can smell its chemicals, and there are no birds. The front entrance says Locked at All Times, and as you skate around the fountain, glance up at the mirrored glass to see your reflection in fun-house mirrors. Number 1401 is square blocks of buildings made of square building blocks; even the glass is square. After you check out number 1401, go back to 1220 and skate all the way to the back of the parking lot behind the building. Through the fence you will see a lovely duck pond, with no straight lines in sight. Living things have such pleasing shapes.

The business park isn't quite completed yet, so after you cross back over to the south side of the street at North Loop Road West, you see some very interesting sand dunes and palm trees. (Also some gang graffiti.) On weekends, the five-star pavement of the parkway is pretty much deserted. If you want a place for the kids to really rip, try this out.

The last mile or so of this trail runs along the south half of Shoreline Park. It is just a gem. Take your time.

Places to Eat

Along this marvelously uninterrupted path around Bay Farm Island, the only place to eat is at the white tablecloths of the restaurant at the Bay Farm Recreation Center.

If you don't mind a bit of a detour, just before the little jog in the trail where you dip under the drawbridge, you can skate all the way across the recreation center parking lot and head west along the sidewalks of Island Drive. Eventually you will come to a shopping center at street level that has pizza and other comestibles. If you look around behind the buildings, you will discover an interesting thing about this island: it's honeycombed with canals. They're fun to skate around, as long as you don't try to go too fast.

Public Transportation

The AC Transit 49 bus runs to the ferry dock, including weekends. You can reach it from Fruitvale BART. The Harbor Bay Ferry operates every day.

Other Trails to Check Out in the Neighborhood

Alameda's Southshore Trail. With perseverance, you can skate from Bay Farm Island to Alameda across the Otis Drive/ Doolittle Drive drawbridge without negotiating any traffic. (Note that CalTrans, the bridge operators, allow pedestrians on the bridge. Skaters are pedestrians.) Head across the parking lot of the Bay Farm Recreation Center and turn left to the bridge. On the other side of the bridge, take a left at the light into a blacktop cul-de-sac. Head toward the shore at the Public Access/Scenic Walk sign and the Public Shore sign. Take a right on the concrete path by the shore, then fork right at the second set of benches, just before the swimming pool. Hang a left on Bayview, and you have made it to the beginning of the Alameda Southshore Trail, with no cross traffic.

Chapter 18

Alameda Creek from Niles to the Bay

Ratings	
Overall Rating	●●●●
Path Surface	●●●
Public Transit Access	●●●●
Surroundings	●●●●●
Level of Difficulty	Easy
Length	Over 12 miles one way

If somebody had asked President Lincoln how long a skating trail should be, he might have said, "Long enough to reach the end." This trail is certainly long enough. If you start at the beginning in Niles and skate all the way to the end at San Francisco Bay—and then skate back again—you will be pretty tired.

How to Get There by Car

To get to the western end of this trail, exit Interstate 880 at Alvarado Boulevard. Take the first right onto Alvarado Boulevard, then a quick left onto Deep Creek Road. After a few blocks, go right on Ariel at Deep Creek Park, past the Ashwood Village sign, then left on Caliban. You'll find some parking on the south side of the street. Look for two signs: No

Dumping and, next to it, an iconic representation of a dog dumping—with a slash through it.

To get to the eastern end of this trail, exit Interstate 880 at the Alvarado-Niles exit in Union City and head east on Alvarado-Niles Road. It's about ten miles from the Alvarado District to the Niles District. Alvarado-Niles Road becomes Niles Boulevard when it gets to Niles. After you cross H Street, I Street, and J Street, be alert for a ninety-degree left turn under a railroad bridge. This is where Niles Boulevard becomes Niles Canyon Road. A block or two after you come out of the tunnel you'll intersect Mission Boulevard. Across the street on the right is a sign announcing Sunol 6, Livermore 17, and also a restaurant called Big Daddy's with a huge parking lot. After you cross Mission Boulevard, on the way to Sunol, the road that wanders off to the right and looks like an extension of Big Daddy's parking lot is Old Canyon Road. Just a few hundred yards down Old Canyon Road is a staging area on the left, at the intersection with Canyon Oaks Court. It's down in a gully and a little hard to spot.

What It's Like

The trail is actually the top of a levee that runs along Alameda Creek. It's spectacularly uneventful for almost its entire twelve-mile length, just a good asphalt surface that passes blissfully under streets and freeways. Some of the underpasses are better engineered than others, but they are all a vast improvement over pushing a little green button on a street light and waiting for the cars to stop.

If you start out at the western end of the trail near Ashwood Village, head up a ramp to the top of the levee and go left. The trail runs a little over four miles with no cross traffic. After you leave the subdivisions behind you'll see some beautiful sugar beet farms off to the left. On the right is what's left of Alameda Creek before it drips into San Francisco Bay. The

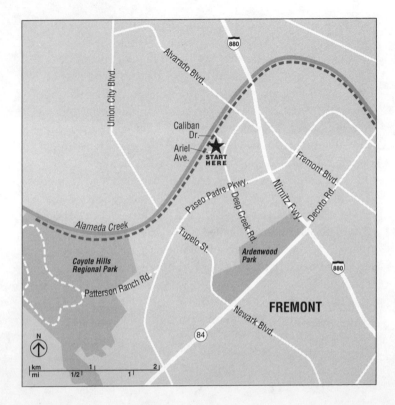

marsh and floodplain are protected from developers and pre-
served unto perpetuity as our defense against excessive rain.

The mile markers on the trail can be confusing for skaters
because they do not measure from the beginning of the pavement. When you get near the east end of the trail, you come
to a blind hairpin turn. Be careful.

That's the end of the flat part of the trail, and it's a good
place to turn back. For those who like to climb hills, you can
head up the rise on the right to a signpost that points left to
Bayview Trail. If you follow that sign, you will end up at the
Visitor Center of Coyote Hills Regional Park.

The eastern end of the trail in Niles is where Charlie
Chaplin had his Essanay movie studio. Check out the

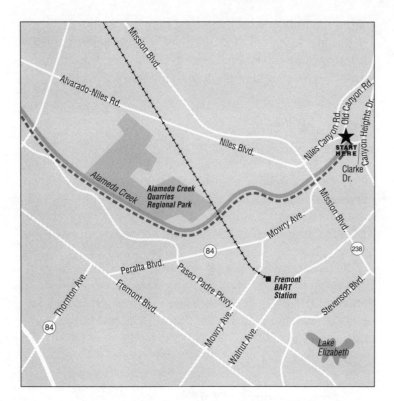

country/western dance hall by the railroad station, the antique stores, Vallejo Mill Historic Park, and the old train station. (There is an Essanay Place in this neighborhood, but it doesn't bear any traces of Chaplin.)

From the staging area west of town, start skating west along Alameda Creek. The trail is good asphalt, not overly smooth but quite serviceable. The only difficulty is in negotiating some of the underpasses, with their steep descents and immediate inclines. After going under Mission Boulevard, you will enjoy a one-mile uninterrupted stretch before you come to a railroad bridge and BART overpass. The next bridge, or sign of civilization, is nearly two miles down the path. Skate this path when you are looking for exercise, not excitement.

Nature abounds to your right, tract homes to your left. As you get within a few miles of the freeway, the surroundings turn more and more urban. The scenery doesn't open up again until the western end of the trail near Ashwood Village.

Places to Eat

Big Daddy's is well known in this area; it's been here at the corner of Mission Boulevard and Niles Canyon Road since 1951. If you're wearing skates, try the outdoor seating. Note, however, that Big Daddy's is an atavism of the fifties, a major-meat barbecue establishment, so you may want to absorb the prevailing attitude of that period and not call much attention to yourself.

If you can still move after eating at Big Daddy's, you can leave your car in the parking lot and skate across Mission Boulevard (Highway 238) at the light. Skate south across the bridge over Alameda Creek. On the opposite side of the bridge, and to your right, is a partly unpaved access to the trail.

Public Transportation

The Niles staging area is served by AC Transit's 26 line. The 26 line goes to Fremont BART.

Other Trails to Check Out in the Neighborhood

Coyote Hills Interpretive Center in Newark

Chapter 19

Coyote Hills Interpretive Center in Newark

Ratings	
Overall Rating	●●●
Path Surface	●●
Public Transit Access	None
Surroundings	●●●●●
Level of Difficulty	Challenging
Length	A loop of about 3 miles

Before the Spanish arrived, the Miwok families living in this area paddled a few yards out into the bay, caught their lunch, took it home, cooked it, ate it, and discarded the shells. After thousands of years of tossing the shells into the same piles, the piles became shell mounds.

Back where I grew up in South Jersey, there was a town about ten or fifteen miles away that was full of professional oyster shuckers. A canning factory just outside of town processed the oysters and built up a remarkable pile of discarded oyster shells. The name of that town is now South Port Norris, but I've never heard anybody call the place anything but Shellpile. Maybe the Miwoks who lived here called their town something like Shellpile.

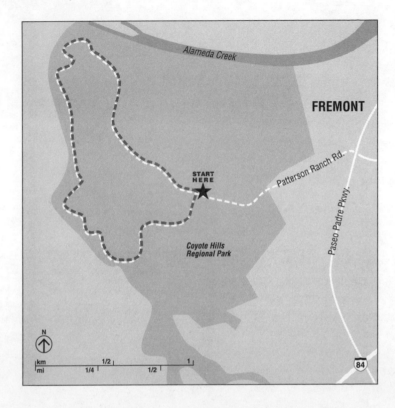

Nearly a hundred years ago, some University of California professors tracked down the few remaining Miwoks and asked them to say a few words. The anthropologist Alfred Kroeber translated an apparently unedited bit of their dialogue: "When low-tide, not can kill rabbits, then you go, when low-tide, then you gather abalones, clams, that you eat-with your acorn-bread" (A. L. Kroeber, "The Chumash and Costanoan Languages," *University of California Publications in American Archaeology and Ethnology* 9, no. 2 [Nov. 19, 1910]: 237–71.) Apparently, every day they could walk out and grab some clams. *That's* peace of mind.

Call the Coyote Hills Regional Park Visitor Center (510-795-9385) to make sure it's open that day.

How to Get There by Car

From Interstate 880, go west on Highway 84 following the signs for Dumbarton Bridge/Highway 84 West. Before you reach the Dumbarton Bridge toll plaza on 84, take the exit Thornton Avenue/Newark. Turn right at the top of the off-ramp and drive north on a road called Paseo Padre (Thornton Avenue is the same road to the south). When you see Patterson Ranch Road heading off to the left, take a left to the park entrance. Drive ahead to the parking lots surrounding the visitor center.

What It's Like

The Coyote Hills trail is a challenging loop around a mountain, with lots of ups and downs, twists and turns, and skating along a steep hillside.

From the visitor center, start skating east through the parking lot. At the end of the lot, the Bayview Trail continues a short distance on the left, then crosses Patterson Ranch Road at the signpost. This is an old, rough section of trail. Skate up to a newer signpost that says To Refuge with a left arrow. The newer pavement here goes gently downhill. Follow the To Shoreline sign. Don't go uphill; the path goes nowhere. Go right; the trail winds around the hill, a slight upgrade. When you get to the other side of the hill, you will be facing the bay.

Occasionally this trail becomes hard to follow, because the little metal plaques disappear from the carved signposts. As you circle the hill, be alert for bicyclists on blind turns. One of the trails to your left takes you directly to the Alameda Creek Trail.

The trail back to the visitor center is partly concrete; stay to the left.

Don't leave the visitor center without stopping in to look around. You'll see a mural of the neighborhood, a video of the Indian site, an operational tule boat, and other wonders.

Places to Eat

The visitor center has no commissary, but they do provide picnic tables.

A few times a year you can eat at Ardenwood Farm, just around the bend from the visitor center. The people at Ardenwood will show and tell you all about the non–Native American food supply.

Public Transportation

None.

Other Trails to Check Out in the Neighborhood

Alameda Creek from Niles to the Bay. This trail actually connects with the Coyote Hills trail, but the connecting link is steep.

Chapter 20

Livermore's Multi-Use Pathway

Ratings	
Overall Rating	●●
Path Surface	●●●; some ● (cobblestones)
Public Transit Access	●●●●
Surroundings	●●
Level of Difficulty	Easy
Length	About 3 miles one way

When you get to the end of this flat, three-mile-long trail, at Almond Avenue in East Livermore, you're skating around the former playing fields of Almond Avenue School. The school was closed by the school board, and the property was leased by the Lawrence Livermore National Laboratory, located just a few miles down the road on East Avenue. But the radiation business hasn't been very good lately, so the Rad Lab has turned part of the former school property (the part not used for child care) into a science-oriented campus for kids. The little departments are labeled pods. Pod F, for example, is a computer museum, the kind of computer museum that could be brought to you only by the lab. It's got a supercomputer—a genuine Cray—and it's located in the same building as the lab's Dosimetry Department, the place where lab workers take their little badges to see if they'd gotten too big a dose of

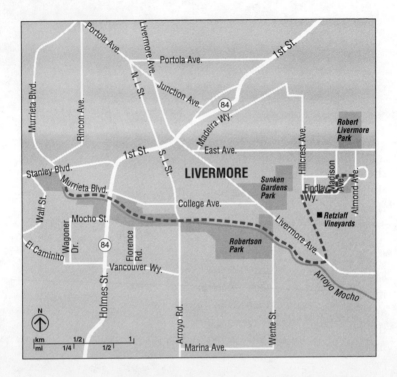

gamma rays. All the buildings are one story, so you can skate right up. Call ahead for a tour of these and other facilities (510-373-1373). You can drop in to the Science Education Center without reservations.

How to Get There by Car

From eastbound Interstate 580, take the Portola Avenue exit. Not too far from the freeway, take the right fork in the road onto North Murrieta Boulevard, a major thoroughfare. Stay on Murrieta until you come to another major thoroughfare, Stanley Boulevard. Look for a shopping center on the left and a gas station on the corner on the right. Turn right onto Stanley and look immediately across the street for the staging area to the right of the gas station. Go to the end of the block, hang a U-turn, and park in that staging area. Despite Livermore's generally bucolic atmosphere, rush hour at Stanley and Murrieta is just as intense as it is in a big city.

If you're westbound on 580, take the First Street exit and go left on First Street. You're on Highway 84. Follow Highway 84 past Livermore Avenue to a three-cornered intersection with Holmes Street. Turn left and go south on Holmes, then take a quick right on Murrieta. You will see a staging area on the other side of the gas station on the southwest corner of the intersection of Murrieta and Stanley Boulevards. Park there.

What It's Like

The trail to the north is brutish and short. Instead, start skating left on the wide smooth asphalt trail next to the staging area. There's a steep underpass and a wooden bridge within the first half mile. After that it's smooth sailing for almost two miles, along a creek, by a horseshoe pit, over a concrete bridge, and then back again—fairly laid back, not very urban. At the fork by the fairgrounds (the site of the annual rodeo), stay to the left.

The path crosses Tesla Road/South Livermore Avenue. Past the massive gate and sign announcing Concannon Vineyards is the auto entrance to Retzlaff Vineyards; skate past it, and look for the skaters' entrance (a deleted section of fencing leading to hard-packed gravel) just after the first sharp left turn. Retzlaff's is open for tasting daily from 12 to 2 and weekends 12 to 5; skaters welcome. As you skate down the path you can inspect the very vines your glass of wine came from. After you go around the vineyard, the trail becomes more urban along Findlay Way. At Hillcrest, jog right after the cobblestone crosswalk, then jog left again at the bench area at Findlay Way and St. Mary Drive. You have to repeat this rather odd drill again at Madison Avenue. At Madison and Findlay go straight, then take a sharp left around Almond Park. The trail ends at Almond Avenue and Almond Circle.

If you skate past the Almond Avenue School site, you can turn around in the five-star parking lot behind the Church of Christ between Almond Court and East Avenue.

Places to Eat

In the Pepper Tree Plaza shopping center at the western end of the trail, at Stanley Boulevard and Murrieta Boulevard, try Liberty Pizza parlor. Go for ice cream next door at Heart's Delight. Both are open seven days a week.

Retzlaff Vineyards (510-447-8941) has picnic tables you may use. Treat yourself to something really special; buy a bottle of Dr. Taylor's merlot.

Public Transportation

The Wheels Route 10 (Livermore/Amador Valley Transit Authority, a local bus service in Pleasanton, Livermore, and Dublin) will take you to the western end of the trail. Weekdays there is BART Express Bus UL to Livermore from BART Walnut Creek. Weekends you have to go to Pleasanton first via BART UP and catch Wheels.

Other Trails to Check Out in the Neighborhood

The Iron Horse Trail

San Francisco

Chapter 21

The Embarcadero

Ratings

Overall Rating	●●●
Path Surface	● (sidewalk); some ●●●●● (piers)
Public Transit Access	●●●●
Surroundings	●●
Level of Difficulty	Easy
Length	2 miles one way

The first clue you'll have that the Embarcadero is a good place to skate is the multitude of lunch-hour skaters who let down their big-city aloofness to wave to you as they whiz by. They belong. You belong. The second clue is that there is easy two-hour parking near the Embarcadero or near Pier 19. Note: Bring along plenty of quarters for the parking meters.

San Francisco has hills so steep they have steps carved into the sidewalks, but down here at the waterfront the pavement is level. This trail is about as urban as it gets, composed almost entirely of very wide sidewalks, but the Embarcadero always sets its own pace. If you take your time with the pedestrians, even beginners can skate an easy two miles.

How to Get There by Car

After you cross the Golden Gate Bridge southbound on Highway 101, follow the signs for Doyle Drive and take a right exit

following the signs for Lombard Street/Downtown. You will be on Richardson Avenue for a short time, then bear left on Lombard. Stay in the left lanes. Where Highway 101 turns right (onto Van Ness Avenue), you should turn left onto Van Ness and then a quick right turn onto Bay Street. Bay Street runs into the Embarcadero at Montgomery Street. Turn right; you can usually find parking across the street, on the bay side of the Embarcadero.

From westbound Interstate 80 and the San Francisco-Oakland Bay Bridge, stay in the left lane of the Bay Bridge and take the first left exit, Main Street, at a conservative pace. After a tight 270-degree turn, stay in the right-hand lane and make the first right, onto Harrison Street. Harrison Street ends at the Embarcadero. Turn left and park anywhere.

If you cruise too far north on the Embarcadero, you will

be in the Fisherman's Wharf area, where parking spaces are at a premium.

What It's Like

From wherever you found a parking spot (or wherever your public conveyance dropped you off), start by skating south along the Embarcadero's wide sidewalk, which runs beside the piers. The Embarcadero wasn't always so sunny and pleasant. Until recently, it was overshadowed by the Embarcadero Freeway, an elevated, hellish monstrosity that ran above the middle of the street. After the earthquake of '89 the city tore it down.

A new promenade is being constructed to extend the path south of Howard Street. If it isn't done yet, and Howard Street still looks like a construction zone, turn around and skate north. Stop for a moment when you get to the stanchion of the Bay Bridge, an object of remarkable bulk and solidity.

The concrete sidewalk path is narrow between Howard Street and the Ferry Building (the building with the clock tower), but it's much skated by the locals. Note the sculpture of two glazed old-fashioned stainless steel doughnuts. San Francisco's fireboats are anchored on your right. Cross the street at Harrison so you can admire the Gordon Biersch brewery tanks in the old Hills Brothers Coffee building. There is a ramp up to the plaza. Beer served to skaters.

Pier 1 (odd-numbered piers are north of Market Street, even-numbered south) is the ferry dock for Alameda and other East Bay ports of call. It has a restaurant open at 6 A.M. for breakfast.

Down by the Ferry Building the Embarcadero is a place of huge piers and small boats. San Francisco doesn't contribute much to the shipping trade anymore. Most of the huge oceangoing vessels gliding by on the bay are container ships headed for Oakland. The left side of Pier 3 is the usual berth for the *Santa Rosa*, a ferry boat from a bygone era. It's okay to skate right up to the plank, any day from 9 A.M. to 6 P.M. Pier 7 is a fishing pier, quiet and lovely but wooden and hard to skate on.

Pier 39 is one of San Francisco's best-known tourist attractions. You can't skate on the boardwalk portions of the pier, but feel free to skate on the excellent pavement all around the pier. Stop to admire the seal sculpture near the sidewalk, and take a look at the live sea lions on the docks as you circumnavigate on five-star concrete. At the end of Pier 39 is a stunning view of Alcatraz.

A little farther west on the Embarcadero, note the so-called cable car tours. The management says you can take a motorized imitation cable car tour with your skates on, if you like.

The end of the trail is at Pier 45, where you see the End Embarcadero and End Taylor signs. Skate out on Pier 45, following the signs to USS *Pampanito*, past the row of telescopes; it's a good trail to a World War II submarine. Sometimes the SS *Jeremiah O'Brien*, the last operational Liberty ship, is berthed at the pier as well. The pier also has a Ripley's Believe It or Not! museum. Off to starboard, you can see the two docks for the Angel Island and Tiburon Ferries, and the tourist ferries to Alcatraz.

The Embarcadero is lit at night. Between Pier 35 and Pier 39 is an abstract sculpture that looks especially good by streetlight.

Places to Eat

At the north end of the Embarcadero, near Pier 43, you can belly up to the Franciscan Crab Stand and order anything from a shrimp cocktail to a full-course meal. They have outdoor tables, and the seafood is as tasty as any along Fisherman's Wharf. A short distance away at Pier 41 is a Ben and

Jerry's ice cream stand. Both places serve excellent espresso.

If you are out for a little night skating, Boudin's Bakery is open late and you can skate through. Excellent meals, excellent pastry, and real sourdough. During the day you can skate up to large plate glass windows and watch them bake.

Public Transportation

Three ferry lines stop at the Ferry Building: Angel Island/ Tiburon Ferry; Golden Gate Ferry to Sausalito and Larkspur; and Alameda/Oakland Ferry (the Blue and Gold fleet). The Red and White fleet puts in at Pier 43.

Amtrak buses stop at the Ferry Building, and several Muni lines (19, 32, 42) stop somewhere along the Embarcadero. Muni 2, 7, 8, 9, 14, 21, and 31 go to the Ferry Building.

From Embarcadero BART you can skate down Market Street to the Ferry Building. Around Christmastime, you will have the pleasure of roller-skating next to an outdoor ice-skating rink as you cross Justin Herman Plaza.

Other Trails to Check Out in the Neighborhood

The Presidio and Marina Green
Golden Gate Park
Ocean Beach

Chapter 22

The Presidio and Marina Green

Ratings	
Overall Rating	●●●
Path Surface	●●●; some ●●●●●
Public Transit Access	●●●●
Surroundings	●●
Level of Difficulty	Easy
Length	2.25 miles one way

You might experience an uneasy feeling along the Presidio and Marina Green Trail—the feeling that it is simply too good to be true. Did the U.S. Army just check out and leave this place to you? There's got to be a catch. But look around. Most of the base is closed, and more of it is closing all the time. The western end of this trail still looks very military, but gradually the Presidio will, like Fort Mason, complete its metamorphosis from sword into plowshare.

If you are particular about grains of sand getting into the running gear of your skates, you should avoid the whole trail. The prevailing winds coming through the Golden Gate leave sand everywhere, even near the marina itself. But if you decide to go for it, you will find two and a quarter miles of flat, easy, shoreline skating.

How to Get There by Car

If you are coming southbound on Highway 101 over the Golden Gate Bridge, follow the 101 South/Downtown and Doyle Drive signs. Stay in the right lane, and follow the Downtown/Lombard Street signs. After a short hop on Richardson Avenue, you'll see a smaller sign for Crissy Field; make a quick 180-degree right turn into the Presidio. You will be on newer pavement, and you'll see one of the towers of the Golden Gate Bridge ahead of you. You are heading back under the freeway on Gorgas Avenue to Mason Street. Go left on Mason about a mile to McDonald. Go right on McDonald, then take a left on Marine Drive to Hamilton Street. Stop. Park anywhere.

Going westbound on Interstate 80 across the Bay Bridge, stay in the right-hand lanes and exit at Highway 101/Golden Gate Bridge. Exit at South Van Ness Avenue. After the excruciating stop-and-go trip north on 101/Van Ness Avenue, make a left turn onto Lombard, a right onto Fillmore (to the end), and a left onto Marina Boulevard. From here to the parking area you will get a preview of the area you'll be skating. Where Marina meets Lyon Street, go straight, with a slight jog to the left. Don't jog too far to the left or you will be transported against your will onto the Golden Gate Bridge and perhaps beyond. The street you should jog onto is Mason Street. Follow Mason Street a mile or so to McDonald, go left on Marine Drive to Hamilton, and park.

What It's Like

The western end of this trail is off to your left, at the end of Hamilton Street. From Hamilton or McDonald Streets, start skating east on the asphalt trail. The trail runs between the parking lots and shuttered military facilities of the Presidio's Crissy Field, and the strip of dunes belonging to Golden Gate National Recreation Area.

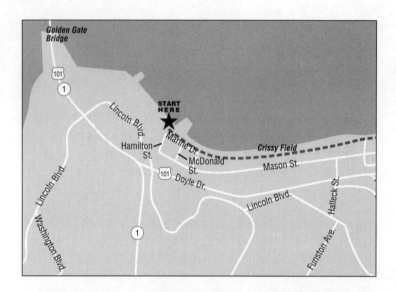

After a little over a mile, go left through West Pipe Gate. The seaside trail turns to dirt and sand here, so head right onto a little paved path to a runway—an aircraft runway! Taxi to the left down the runway to a large paved parking lot. Go right at the parking lot, and you will see a new asphalt trail to your left. Follow this trail through the gate at Lyon Street to the Marina Green.

All of the red-tinted five-star concrete surrounding the Marina Green is off-limits to skaters. It is also off-limits to bicyclists and skateboarders. Drivers do, however, park right under the No Roller-Skating signs, put on their skates, and roll right along, next to all the bicyclists and a few skateboarders. (Jogging, by the way, is allowed.) Law-abiding folks are consigned to the alternate path, turning left on Marina Green Drive at Scott Street and staying close to the water all the way around the bend to the entrance to Fort Mason. Keep to the left as you approach Fort Mason, and skate through the gate at the end of Laguna Street.

You can skate all around the piers here in Fort Mason, ex-

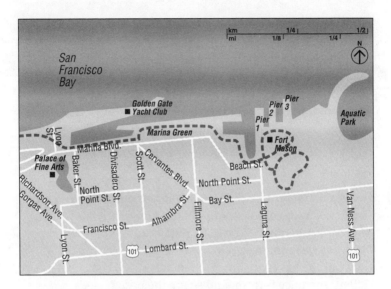

cept the last one, which is called the Festival Pavilion. This is
the pier where the SS *Jeremiah O'Brien* normally resides. The
management of Fort Mason has filled in all the old hazards
such as the railroad tracks, so it is nearly impossible to trip
over them. Skating around the pier building labeled Herbst
Pavilion is especially pleasant. Inside this pier, which is truly
immense and could accommodate the cargo of the most massive of oceangoing vessels, is a spiffy new theater of four hundred or so seats on the concrete ground floor. You can see
the lobby when you skate around on the port side of the
pier. In addition to the large theater in Herbst Pavilion,
called the Cowell Theater, Fort Mason houses two theaters
in Building D run by the Magic Theater, and also the Bayfront Theater. There are almost as many theaters here as in
the theater district near Union Square, and you are much
more likely to see a world premiere here than you are downtown.

So far, this trail has been level. After you have checked
out Fort Mason, if you want to do a little uphill skating, head

back out the main gate and left up Laguna Street. Go about
half a block, and skate up the hill into a park on a five-star
red-tinted concrete path. This park has a Bufano sculpture at
the east end that you can skate up to, and also a statue of the
late Congressman Phil Burton. The trail past the Bufano will
take you down to the Hyde Street Pier, but it's too steep for
skating.

Places to Eat

Green's Restaurant (415-771-6222) is at the far western end of
the Fort Mason complex, in Building A, near the Museum of
Modern Art Rental Gallery. The restaurant is world renowned,
but what we're interested in is the takeout department, which
they call the bakery counter (open at 8 A.M.). The coffee is excellent, the juice is fresh, and so are the baked goods and
sandwiches and other prepared foods. There is a convenient
pay phone. You will have to negotiate a few steps inside the
restaurant, but they're carpeted. You can take your food down
to the piers, to sit on the park benches, or over to the south
end of Building B to the picnic tables.

Places to Rent Skates

Nuvo Colours (415-771-6886) is within skating distance on
Fillmore. Achilles Wheels (415-567-8400) is on Chestnut near
Scott.

Public Transportation

You can take the Muni 29/Sunset bus to Crissy Field. Or you
can take the Muni 22, 28, 30, 42, 47, or 49 lines to the vicin-
ity of Fort Mason National Park Headquarters.

Other Trails to Check Out in the Neighborhood

The Embarcadero
Ocean Beach
Golden Gate Park

Chapter 23

Golden Gate Park

Ratings

Overall Rating	●●●
Path Surface	●●●
Public Transit Access	●●●●
Surroundings	●●●● (Sunday only)
Level of Difficulty	Medium (a few hills)
Length	Almost 2 miles one way

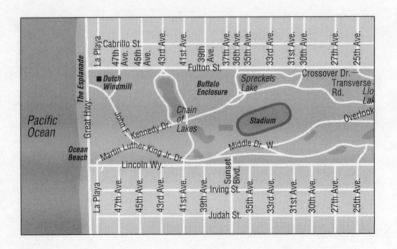

Roller-skating was the rage in San Francisco in the seventies. Droves of people skated in Golden Gate Park, where the land was flat and the skating was easy. Skates were rented out of buses on Fulton Street, Clement Street, and Stanyan Street. Each one of those buses held a hundred pairs of skates or more, and every Sunday they were all rented out. With so many operators, the rates were cheap, which brought more and more people out to skate. Eventually John F. Kennedy Drive was crowded with skaters. An ordinance was passed banning vehicular traffic on the drive from 6 A.M. to 6 P.M. on Sundays between Stanyan Street and Nineteenth Avenue. It was skate heaven. Art and commerce flourished. People exercised and were invigorated, and a spirit of camaraderie filled the park.

Then, just as the whole thing was legislated into existence, it was legislated out of existence. New laws required the fly-by-night rental shops to find permanent roosts with storefronts, business licenses, and—the requirement most burden-

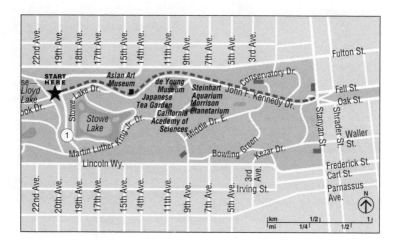

some to freewheeling entrepreneurship—insurance. So one by one the owner-operator skate rental shops went away, and gradually the popularity of Sunday skating in the park declined. No doubt one of these days someone will call the San Francisco Board of Supervisors' attention to the plight of motorists on the drive, and car-less Sunday skating and biking will be a fond memory (like Playland at the Beach). Until that happens, though, John F. Kennedy Drive on Sundays is a great place to skate.

How to Get There by Car

Southbound Highway 101 enters San Francisco over the Golden Gate Bridge. Take the right exit that says Downtown/Lombard Street, and follow southbound 101 as it wends its way through town first as Richardson Avenue, then as it hooks left about 135 degrees to join Lombard Street, and finally turns right (south) on Van Ness Avenue. Drive south about a mile and a half (thirty blocks) to McAllister Street. When you get to McAllister, go right. Go left on Laguna, drive one block, then turn right on Fulton Street. Travel all the way out to Twenty-fifth Avenue, and turn left into Golden Gate Park. Stay to your right, and quickly take the right fork where Cross Over Drive rises up on the left and Transverse Road stays flat on the right. After a twist and turn or two, Transverse Road crosses John F. Kennedy Drive. There is usually parking available near this intersection; take a spot just before the intersection if you can. (Note: There is a quicker route down Highway 1, but I don't find it to be very well marked.)

If you are traveling west on Interstate 80 across the Bay Bridge, stay in the right-hand lanes after you cross the bridge, and take the exit marked Highway 101 North/Golden Gate Bridge.

If you are northbound on Highway 101 from San Francisco International Airport or from San Jose, stay in the left-hand lanes and take the Highway 101 North/Golden Gate Bridge exit.

Once you are on the double-decker elevated freeway that is Highway 101, stay in the left lanes until the Fell/Laguna Street exit. At the bottom of the off-ramp, merge slightly left onto Fell Street. Drive on Fell Street all the way to Stanyan Street, turn right, then go left on Fulton Street. Take Fulton to Twenty-fifth Avenue, and go left into Golden Gate Park. Stay to your right, park anywhere, and skate the last block or two to the barricades the San Francisco Police Department puts up on Sundays at the intersection of Transverse Road and John F. Kennedy Drive.

Note: Parking is difficult (and occasionally unpleasant) at the other end of the trail near Stanyan Street.

What It's Like

Skating in Golden Gate Park Monday through Saturday is only moderately rewarding and somewhat life threatening. At commute time a lot of cars pass through the park, and they're moving fast; at other times, sightseers are wandering through. Then there is the problem of where to skate. The park administration has stenciled "no this" and "no that" on many paths leading to flower gardens and tree groves and statuary and on paths that parallel the streets.

On Sunday, however, the barricades along John F. Kennedy Drive at the Stanyan Street end in the east and at Transverse Road to the west allow skaters a mile and a half of well-maintained asphalt roadway. For many people in the city, it's *the* place to skate.

From where you parked, start skating east on JFK Drive. This moderate incline is about as steep as any of the ups and downs in the park. The road curves past a small lake with a functioning waterfall, and then by a meadow on the right, about a half mile from where you started. In this meadow on some Sundays you can attend free Shakespeare in the Park. If this were back in the Bard's day, the actors would no doubt have a line or two ready for the skaters, maybe something like ". . . if like a crab you could go backward."

There used to be (and sometimes still is) a lot of action near the entrance to the Music Concourse, the circular drive that goes past the de Young Museum, the Asian Art Museum, the band shell, the California Academy of Sciences, the Steinhart Aquarium, and the Morrison Planetarium. At the entrance, which is about three-quarters of a mile from where you started, you might see some ensemble skate dancing and slalom events, and occasionally a ramp for jumps. Skates are not allowed on the Music Concourse itself. That's too bad, because it has a number of interesting outdoor sculptures.

You can skate up and down Conservatory Drive, by the Strybing Arboretum and the Hall of Flowers. Watch for signs stenciled on the pavement telling you where you can skate.

When you get to the eastern barricades at Stanyan Street, it is possible to extend your trip by crossing the street into the Panhandle, which is also parklike. However, all the traffic being diverted from the park is going by on Stanyan Street, so it's not an easy street to cross.

Back at the western barricades, you can skate another interesting mile and a half on JFK Drive out to the ocean. You have to skate in the street with the traffic, though, because the path next to the street is marked No Roller Skates in several places.

The path from Nineteenth Avenue out to Ocean Beach is all slightly downhill. That's fun. After only half a block, you come to a picturesque series of ponds on Chain of Lakes Drive. There is Lloyd Lake and Spreckels Lake, which comes complete with ducks and model boats. When you see signs that say, for example, Beach/36th Avenue, always opt for the beach. There are one or two stop signs.

Places to Eat

Sometimes on Sundays fast-food operators set up their stands by the Music Concourse entrance. Food at the Mexican stand is pretty good.

Out on Fulton Street, near the Tenth Avenue entrance to the park, you can usually find one or two fresh fruit and vegetable merchants.

Places to Rent Skates

Haight Street is just across the street from the park at the eastern end, two blocks up from JFK Drive on Stanyan Street. On the first block of Haight is a skate shop called Skates on Haight, which has been around since the Summer of Love, which was a long time ago. What we've got now is a store with a bad attitude in a bad neighborhood. On the avenues both north and south of the park you'll find skate-rental places that are a lot easier to deal with: Skate Pro at 27th and Irving (415-752-8776); Magic Skates, 3038 Fulton at Sixth Avenue (415-668-1117).

Public Transportation

The San Francisco Municipal Railway will take you to Golden Gate Park, even on Sundays. The Muni 44 line from Clement Street stops at the Music Concourse on the way to the Glen Park BART station. The 29 line goes right to the western barricades on its way to Balboa BART from the marina. The 5 line runs along Fulton Street (the northern boundary of the park) all the way to the downtown BART stations. Best of all is Muni's N-Judah streetcar, because you can take it to Nineteenth Avenue near Irving Street, by the 19th Avenue Diner. If you've never visited San Francisco's Sunset District, you will find this part of it to be very lively.

Other Trails to Check Out in the Neighborhood

Ocean Beach
The Presidio and Marina Green. The Muni 29 line can take you directly to Golden Gate Park from Mason Street near Crissy Field.

Chapter 24

Ocean Beach

Ratings

Overall Rating	●●●●
Path Surface	●●●●; ● (Esplanade)
Public Transit Access	●●●●
Surroundings	●●●●
Level of Difficulty	Easy
Length	3 miles one way

When the wind is blowing in hard off the Pacific and the air is cold and damp, you can remember the few days in the fall when it was balmy and calm in San Francisco and you headed out to Ocean Beach. On a warm day or a warm night you might see hundreds of people on the beach or strolling on the Esplanade. This is the former site of Playland at the Beach and the Sutro Baths. Before Disneyland, families came here.

When you go to Ocean Beach to skate, remember to bring along a few layers of warm clothes. Just in case.

How to Get There by Car

If you are crossing the Golden Gate Bridge southbound on Highway 101, stay in the right-hand lane over the bridge and take the Lincoln Boulevard/Highway 1 exit. Lincoln Boulevard winds up and down through the Presidio and part of the Golden Gate National Recreation Area. At the intersection

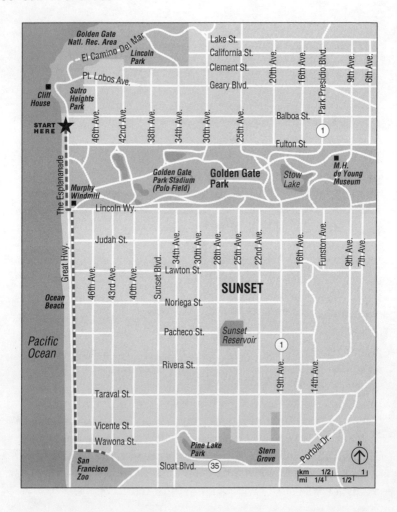

with Twenty-fifth Avenue, go straight. You are now on El
Camino Del Mar—very scenic. After the road makes a sharp
left, you come to the intersection with Point Lobos Avenue.
Turn right on Point Lobos and start the descent to the beach.
The Cliff House is on the right. Cruise down the hill to the
Great Highway and park anywhere on the beach side of the
street.

If you are northbound on Highway 101, take the Highway 101 North/Golden Gate Bridge exit. Then take the Fell/Laguna exit, and drive west on Fell Street all the way to Stanyan Street. Turn right on Stanyan, then left on Fulton Street. Take Fulton Street to its end, at the ocean.

What It's Like

The first mile of this trail at the north end is the wide concrete path, leading to the beach, that is usually called the Esplanade. Skate south, starting at the Point Lobos/Great Highway sign. The concrete is in poor condition but still okay for skating. The view of the Pacific Ocean is magnificent, and Golden Gate Park is on your left.

Where Fulton Street meets the ocean, note the Dutch windmill on your left, and a little farther on, the Murphy windmill. Just past this second windmill is Lincoln Way. Cross the Great Highway at Lincoln, and you will see a well-designed skating trail running north-south on the left side of the road. You can follow it for a little over two miles. Here you lose most of the magnificent view of the Pacific, but you gain a late-model asphalt surface with very little pedestrian traffic and only a few bicycles. On particularly nice days there are lots of skaters. The trail is straight with a few interesting ups and downs.

The asphalt trail ends at Sloat Boulevard. If you continue south on the concrete sidewalk, you will see some concrete artwork at the Westside Pump Station. The parklike area across the street on your left is the zoo. (No skating in the zoo.) Across the street leading to the beach are extensive parking lots for viewing the ocean.

When you get back up to the north end of the trail by Fulton Street, take a look at the steep incline to the Cliff House. If you think you can negotiate it, go up the Esplanade and follow the signs to the Musée Mechanique. The concrete path leads to a spectacular overlook generally known as Seal Rocks. Most days you can see surfers out beyond the rocks. The Musée Mechanique, tucked under the hotel on your right, is a marvelous collection of old contrivances, including a Wurlitzer mechanical piano that you can see from the window. An old sign says No Skates, but the person dispensing change to operate the machines is sometimes rolling around on skates himself. In the back are the more recent crunch-and-punch video games.

The Golden Gate National Recreation Area Visitor's Center is just across the terrace from the museum. The Camera Obscura on the south side of the terrace looks like a tourist-trap attraction, but it is worth the price of admission. Take the time to read the information plaques here and there around the plaza; they impart some of the flavor of what this area was like not that long ago, when Playland at the Beach and the Sutro Baths were still in operation.

Places to Eat

A little over a mile from where you started by the Cliff House, you can spot the turnaround for Muni's N-Judah streetcar at Judah and La Playa. After you negotiate the ramp from the trail down to the street, you can skate into Java Beach, a low-key little restaurant dedicated to coffee. You might especially appreciate the display of aerial photographs of San Francisco, from a book with commentary by Herb Caen, columnist for the *San Francisco Chronicle*. This place has a very diverse clientele; it used to be a bar known euphemistically as Dick's Coffee Shop.

At the south end of the trail, across from the entrance to the zoo on the south side of Sloat, you'll find a few walk-up restaurants straight out of the fifties. You can skate to them easily.

Places to Rent Skates

Try the End of the Line Skate Shop, a mile and a half south and one block east of the trail, on Taraval Street at the corner of Forty-seventh and Taraval, open 11 to 7 every day (415-566-7087). This is a real laid-back place, but quite competent and knowledgeable with reasonable rental rates.

Roller-skating need not involve you in any grease or bearings or wrenches or even any concern about such things. A shop like this one can take care of all that. Just ask them to rotate the wheels and check out the bearings. It's impressive to watch a skilled mechanic's hand spin a wheel on a skate (or a farm tractor) and say, "Feel that rough spot? Right there," or "Feels okay to me," or "Cheap bearings."

Public Transportation

The Great Highway trail is the end of the line of two San Francisco Municipal Railway streetcar lines. Either the L-Taraval or the N-Judah will take you there. Sometimes in the summer and fall the Muni adds special open-air cars to these lines.

The Muni 18 bus runs parallel to the trail on Forty-sixth Avenue, two and a half blocks east of the trail. If you get tired you can ride it back to where you started near Fulton Street. (Note: Muni drivers aren't supposed to let you ride with skates on, nor are they supposed to let you ride barefoot. Bring moccasins.)

The Muni 5, 23, 31, 38, 48, and 71 lines also go to Ocean Beach.

Other Trails to Check Out in the Neighborhood

Golden Gate Park
The Presidio and Marina Green

South Bay

Chapter 25

San Mateo County

Ratings

Overall Rating ●●●●
Path Surface ●●●●
Public Transit Access ●●●●
Surroundings ●●●● for long stretches
Level of Difficulty Easy
Length 8 miles one way

Overall Rating ●●●●
Path Surface ●●●
Public Transit Access None
Surroundings ●●●●
Level of Difficulty Easy (the south end); challenging (the north end)
Length 6 miles one way

Highway 92 starts in Alameda County, crosses San Francisco Bay as the San Mateo Bridge, and runs all the way across San Mateo County on the way to the shores of Half Moon Bay. On its way across the county, Highway 92 intersects two first-class roller-skating trails.

Where the San Mateo Bridge touches shore in Foster City, Highway 92 crosses the eight-mile Shoreline Trail in San

Mateo. This trail extends from Coyote Point up by the airport, past Little Coyote Point just north of the San Mateo Bridge, to Sea Cloud Park in Foster City several miles south of the bridge. Someday this flat stretch of asphalt along the marshy tidelands will be connected with similar stretches of pavement all the way around San Francisco Bay to form the Bay Trail.

Several miles across San Mateo County, Highway 92 nearly crosses another exceptional skating trail of a different sort altogether. Sawyer's Camp Trail is up in the hills, over six miles long, with lots of twists and turns and switchbacks and a definite grade from beginning to end. At the south end, toward Pacifica, the trail is relatively tame—an excellent choice for family outings. You can go four miles or more and turn back anytime it feels like too much of a climb. At the north end, though, it's what you might call a challenge.

Suppose one or two members of your group are just itching to try something challenging. Well, dump them at the north end of Sawyer's Camp Trail, up at Hillcrest Boulevard. Inspect everybody's brake pads, and then let them have at it. It's fun. The rest of the group can drive to the tame, south end, and you can meet somewhere in the middle.

Shoreline Trail

How to Get There by Car

Exit Interstate 880, northbound or southbound, at San Mateo Bridge/Highway 92 West, crossing the bay on the San Mateo Bridge; on the west side of the bay, this highway is called the J. Arthur Younger Freeway. After crossing the bridge, take the first exit, Foster City Boulevard. The bottom of the off-ramp is Chess Drive; take a right on Chess and then a left on Foster

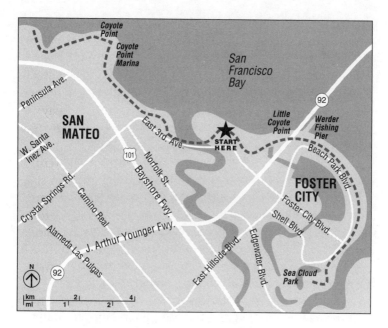

City Boulevard. Go two blocks and park anywhere near the T-intersection of Foster City Boulevard and East Third Street. The trail is between you and the bay, on a levee a few feet above you. It's usually fairly empty.

What It's Like

The Shoreline Trail is remarkable for its length, not its complexity. Start skating from anywhere along East Third Avenue, where the trail approaches obliquely. Note that East Third Avenue stops abruptly a few hundred yards from where you start. If you head south, the trail makes an interesting meander under the San Mateo Bridge. Have faith and follow the arrows. Just on the other side of the bridge, you will see a vestigial bridge, which has evolved into a fishing pier and quasi-marine skating path. The trail continues to the south, along a Foster City street called Beach Park Boulevard. It gets interesting where the path diverges from the street far enough to meld a bit with Belmont Slough. The slough resembles a marsh, but, of course, if it were really a marsh, you wouldn't be skating in it. The path ends at Sea Cloud Park, not far from where Marine World used to be.

You may have enjoyed smooth sailing down to here and ascribed the easy riding to the pavement, which is pretty good asphalt. When you turn around to go back, though, you'll probably notice that the wind was very much at your back. South of the San Mateo Bridge it blows very persistently on occasion. Forewarned is forearmed.

On your way back, when you round the corner of Little Coyote Point, just after the bridge, and get back to East Third Avenue, you might want to stop for lunch at the only deli within reach of the trail, the Lincoln Deli in Lincoln Center on Lincoln Center Drive.

If you want to put off lunch until later, hit the trail again headed north. The wide smooth asphalt goes on for miles, now hugging the shore, now drifting off a hundred yards to sea, for a moment even impersonating a concrete bridge span—an old one, at that—pointing northward to Coyote Point. The shore gets dark and mucky, trying to return to a primordial state. Mile after mile, the trail winds toward the north, the furthest thing from a straight line between these two Points.

Where it almost melds with the beach habitat of the local burrowing owls—just when you're starting to root for nature in earnest—the trail is interrupted by a marina full of boats, a bathing beach, and a concrete structure dedicated to the study of ecology, the Coyote Point Museum. Disregard it all, and skate around the point past the Humane Society, where the airplanes are making their final approach to SFO.

Sawyer's Camp Trail

How to Get There by Car

Get back on Highway 92 in Foster City and take Highway 92 about six miles west, across town. Exit Highway 92 and go north on Interstate 280 to the Millbrae Avenue/Hillcrest Boulevard exit. After you get off the freeway, you have to drive parallel to the freeway for a half mile or so on Skyline Boulevard to Hillcrest Boulevard, turn left, and cross under the freeway on an extension of Hillcrest. At the trailhead, the

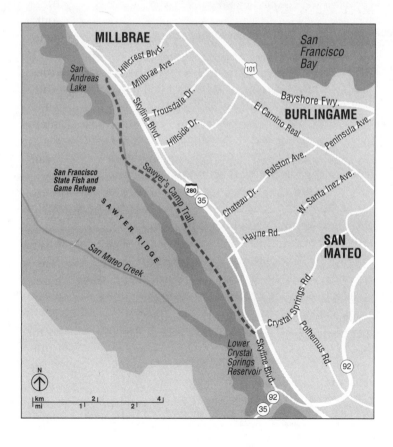

San Mateo Parks and Recreation Department specifically welcomes skaters to the trail.

To get to the south end of the trail, follow signs for Half Moon Bay from Highway 92. After passing Interstate 280, Highway 92 twists to the north and then veers to the west. Just where 92 seems to be taking you off to Half Moon Bay, take a right onto Highway 35 north, which is Skyline Boulevard. After about two miles you will see the trailhead. It's that group of people and cars milling about on your left.

What It's Like

Officially, it's the Sawyer's Camp Trail Multi-Use Pathway, 6.2 miles in length, in the unincorporated area just west of Hillsborough. It's all that's left of what was once the main drag from San Francisco. Now Interstate 280 is the main drag, with Skyline Boulevard the missing link from the vestigial path to the thundering throughway.

From the north end, the numerous plaques and commemorative rocks make this trail a fascinating downhill ride through the history of water in San Francisco. There is one very long downhill stretch across a bridge, with an abrupt turn at the end. It's a left turn. Life is much less terrifying if you know your direction before you start.

One of the former names for this trail, back when it was a highway, was San Andreas Valley Road. This is the legendary seismic hot spot for Northern California; you can see lots of evidence of geologic activity if you look carefully at the rocks along the San Andreas Fault while you skate downhill, mostly here at the north end of the trail. Sometimes the rocks just don't "match up."

From the south end, this trail is a relaxing jaunt along a river. Start skating north from the lower portal to the trail. Try not to do this in the afternoon on a hot summer day, because the sealer that was applied to the cracks in the pavement gets gummy.

For four miles or so, this trail twists and winds along Sawyer Ridge on the way to San Andreas Lake. It's all slightly uphill. The public lands you pass through are quite scenic. When you pass the four-mile marker, Sawyer's Camp Trail gets a little too steep for skating.

Places to Eat

Try the Lincoln Deli along the Shoreline Trail, just about where East Third Avenue grinds to a halt (closed on Sundays).

Around the corner from the Shoreline Trail in San Mateo is a shopping mall called Fashion Island. It's located on Mariner's Island, a little way down Chess Drive from Foster City Boulevard. Fashion Island is widely reputed to have hit the skids because nobody could figure out how to get to it. Most of it is now closed, and plans are afoot to turn it into a cluster of outlet stores. Now, you can find a decent lunch there quite cheap and watch the good-sized crowd of people ice-skating around the rink in the middle of the mall. And then you can walk over to the General Cinema multiplex—a real movie house—and watch a first-run movie for $1.50 per person.

The Sawyer's Camp Trail has no stores along it.

Public Transportation

San Mateo Transit 47F will take you to Third Avenue by the Shoreline Trail.

Other Trails to Check Out in the Neighborhood

St. Francis by the Beach. If you go eight miles west on Highway 92, past the turnoff on Highway 280 that took you to the north end of Sawyer's Camp Trail, you will eventually come to the town of Half Moon Bay on the Pacific Ocean. A little trail here runs north about 2.5 miles from Kelly Street in Half Moon Bay, parallel to the shore, to Miramar Beach. The easiest way to find this trail is to turn right at the corner where Highway 92 runs into Highway 1, and head north to Venice State Beach. Turn left at the access road for Venice State Beach and have a look at the trail, which crosses the access road just a few feet before the park ranger's kiosk. The trail is intended for hikers and equestrians, and the pavement is in bad shape. The scenery by the beach is of course spectacular.

To get something to eat near this trail, drive a few miles north from Half Moon Bay on Highway 1, and turn left at the El Granada stoplight onto Capistrano Road, into the little town of Princeton-by-the-Sea. Take the first quick left into the parking lots of Pillar Point Harbor. Look for Ketch Joanne's Fish Market and Captain's Deck, 25 Johnson Pier (415-728-5959, closed Tues.). Best seafood on earth. And the street skating around town is pretty good, too.

Chapter 26

Los Gatos Creek

<table>
<tr><td colspan="2">**Ratings**</td></tr>
<tr><td>Overall Rating</td><td>●●</td></tr>
<tr><td>Path Surface</td><td>●●; some ●●●</td></tr>
<tr><td>Public Transit Access</td><td>●●●●</td></tr>
<tr><td>Surroundings</td><td>●●●</td></tr>
<tr><td>Level of Difficulty</td><td>Easy north of Camden Dam; challenging to the south</td></tr>
<tr><td>Length</td><td>About 6 miles one way</td></tr>
</table>

The Los Gatos Creek Trail is a locals-oriented recreation trail that has a lot of personality along its six miles. It you might want to take a whole day and get to know better. The first time you see Vasona Reservoir in Vasona Lake Park, for example, you will be surprised at how nice a local city park can be. And skating around Vasona Lake is perfect for beginners and kids.

How to Get There by Car

Follow Interstate 880, south of the junction with Interstate 280 in San Jose, until it becomes Highway 17. Exit Highway 17 at Hamilton Avenue, turning east on Hamilton. Go one long block to South Bascom Avenue and take a right, traveling south on Bascom. Go around the back of the Pruneyard shopping center with a right on East Campbell Avenue. This

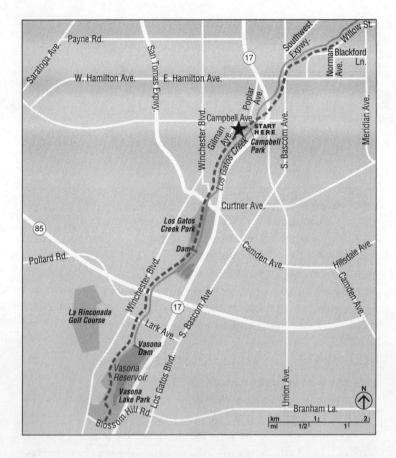

takes you under the freeway. Go past the Campbell Inn, past Poplar Avenue, and at the unsigned intersection with Gilman take a left at the stoplight. When you see the Par Course Parking sign, take a left into a free parking lot. You are in the parking area of Campbell Park.

What It's Like

The whole trail is very parklike. You start off by the playground and picnic grounds of Campbell Park, where a ramp leads up to street level. Take it up to Campbell Avenue, and turn right, across the bridge, to the other side of Los Gatos Creek. Turn down the ramp on the other side, and make a 180-degree turn to your right. You are now on the trail going north, headed out of Campbell toward San Jose.

This part of the trail is uncrowded even on Sunday mornings. It's all underpasses, under South Bascom and a number of other heavily traveled thoroughfares. The pavement is quite good asphalt. After you cross under Hamilton Avenue and get into San Jose's city limits, it's even landscaped.

The landscaped trail is proudly marked with posts bearing the insignia Los Gatos Creek Trail/City of San Jose Trail System. Note that this section of the trail includes a number of underpasses that were hard to build. The cantilevered one near Apple Computer's Campbell Campus is especially noteworthy.

This beautiful project ends all too soon at Willow Street and Norman Avenue, near Leigh Avenue and Hamilton. Turn around and head back.

When you get back to Campbell Park, if you want to skate some more, you can head south on either side of the creek on levee roads that are actually Santa Clara Valley Water District service roads. Whichever side of the creek you are on, be prepared to negotiate a steep hill and a bicycle maze when you get to the first big dam. This might even be a good place to turn around if you have little kids. They will already have covered about six miles on the north end of the trail.

The trail continues south on the western side of the creek, running between an urban park and the freeway. You will encounter some bad pavement. You are now in Los Gatos, cruising through a part of town called Vasona Junction, on pavement that varies from smooth to bad. Just before Lark Avenue comes the sign Steep Hill. Exit the trail and go up to Lark (too steep here), cross the street carefully in the middle of the block (or cross at the light way down at La Canada

Court), and get back on the trail on the eastern side of the creek, still going east.

After an amazing hairpin turn at the top of a hill, you're in Vasona Lake Park at Vasona Reservoir. This is a terrific city park; there are little trails that go off to the sides, leading to ponds with swans, a kids' railroad, and public rest rooms. Our trail lies across the street from the lake to the left. Follow the crosswalk. There is no automobile traffic.

The trail ends at Blossom Hill Road, ahead to the left of the lake. It may be a bit confusing, because a vestigial end of the trail lies further ahead and even has an underpass for Blossom Hill. That little paved fossil doesn't go anywhere just now, though in the future it will go all the way to St. Joseph's College.

Places to Eat

At the north end of the trail, across the intersection from the Classic Carwash with the riverboat motif, you will find a pair of eating establishments clustered together in the middle of the Hamilton Plaza shopping center like binary stars. You have the Bread of Life Alternative Food Store. It carries bulk stuff on the outside, very cheap; pricey stuff on the inside, like organic meat and veggies; and a sandwich counter. Maybe because of the aura of wholesomeness that pervades the place, everything tastes wonderful. Roll on in. Next door is a Starbucks coffee shop. You can spend some of your wholesome aura on a dose of caffeine and pastry.

Public Transportation

The Santa Clara County Transportation Agency SCCTA 27 line stops where the Los Gatos Trail ends, at Blossom Hill Road near Roberts Road. The 63 line stops near the beginning of the trail.

San Jose has an extensive public transit system, including a help line at 408-370-9191 for information about Los Gatos.

Other Trails to Check Out in the Neighborhood

Bayfront Park Recreation Trail in Menlo Park. Take the Marsh Road exit from Highway 101 in Menlo Park. The entrance to Bayfront Park lies a few hundred feet north of the freeway, where the Bayfront Expressway turns into Haven Avenue. Just before you enter Bayfront Park, look for a skating trail running east.

The trail runs parallel and adjacent to the Bayfront Expressway for a mile and a half. When the trail approaches Willow Road, it hooks to the left through a marsh and quiets down for a very pleasant spell, which ends at a staging area just off Highway 84; then it reappears on the northbound side of Highway 84 (the approach to the Dumbarton Bridge). Now this is the truly interesting part: if you cross Highway 84, you can continue on that trail on the northbound side, heading to your left, toward the bay. You can then skate all the way to the Dumbarton Bridge. You can even skate over the bridge, although be warned that it is a steep, narrow, concrete challenge. (According to Bill Bassett of CalTrans's legal department (916-651-2852), a skater is a pedestrian and may traverse a CalTrans bridge anywhere a pedestrian may. Note that the Golden Gate Bridge is not a CalTrans bridge.)

You can then skate for several miles farther on a completely unused road parallel to Highway 84 on the other side of the bridge. You can skate nearly as far as the toll plaza several miles away. Unfortunately, most of this is next to a noisy highway.

Shoreline Amphitheater Trail System in Mountain View. Like the Bayfront trail above, this trail is a mere hop, skip, and a jump from the freeway. Take the San Antonio Road exit from Highway 101 and follow the signs to San Antonio Road North. Drive two short blocks north on San Antonio Road, where it comes to an end at the intersection with Terminal Boulevard. Park anywhere. Look for a green painted gate and a smooth asphalt trail leading north to a handsome interpretive plaque announcing that this is a nature trail. You can see Shoreline Amphitheater from here.

As Yogi Berra once said, "When you come to a fork in the road, take it." A short distance farther north of the plaque along this trail, you come to the fork that clarifies the catcher's remark even further. The leftmost tine of the fork is a trail about one mile long through a picturesque marsh. (A continuation of the trail next to Adobe Creek is closed part of the year.)

It was indeed paved as a trail, not as a road; it's smooth, albeit fissured. The middle tine is unpaved; forget it. The rightmost fork heads off toward the amphitheater, the golf course, and even the movie multiplex miles away, but after only a half mile or so the pavement (left over from this area's days as a dump) turns rough and granular, with sand scattered on the asphalt for good measure. The surroundings rate at least four stars, five if you're into swamps.

In addition to the asphalt trails through the marshland, you can also find several miles of concrete paths nearby, threaded through the deluxe campuses of some of Silicon Valley's heaviest hitters, all within a stone's throw of Shoreline Amphitheater.

Chapter 27

Coyote Creek Trail

Ratings

Overall Rating	●●●●
Path Surface	●●●●; some ●●●
Public Transit Access	●●●
Surroundings	●●●●
Level of Difficulty	Easy
Length	10 miles

The first time you venture onto the Coyote Creek Trail, you will be amazed that you didn't try it out years ago. This trail parallels Highway 101, and everyone who has driven up and down Highway 101 has passed within a few hundred yards of it, but few people from outside San Jose know about it and enjoy it. It's pleasant, relaxing, and bucolic for most of its ten or so miles, and it's no problem for beginners.

In some places the Coyote Creek Trail is ideal: quiet, smooth, and easy to skate on, surrounded by trees and fields. In at least one or two places, it is a public servant's nightmare, ravished by graffiti and underfunded for maintenance.

How to Get There by Car

Take the Cochrane Road exit off Highway 101 (the South Valley Freeway) in Morgan Hill, and head west on Cochrane Road. Turn right on Monterey Highway, which is Business

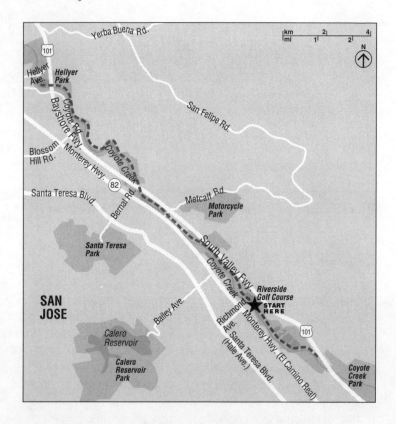

Route 101, and which was formerly State Highway 101. Take
your time; since the new freeway went through, this stretch
of road is pretty sleepy. After going north a little over two
miles you will see a sign directing you to Riverside Golf
Course, to the right. Take the right turn, and after about a half
mile, you will see the trail on your right. Drive a little farther,
and you will see the trail again, protected by some concrete
parking-lot pylons. Park by the electric substation and put on
your skates.

What It's Like

From the electric substation, you can skate for two miles south, through brushland, on a curving strip of smooth asphalt. Round-trip, that's a nice four-plus-mile excursion. Or you can go north, bearing in mind that the trail runs over ten miles that way, and the best part was where you started.

When you head north, the first mile or so lies above a dry underground stream. Then you find yourself in a beautiful riparian environment, on a great trail with a distinctively rural milieu—for miles there are no cross streets. Then the trail dumps you onto a dead-end street, just opposite the South County Schutzhund Club. Skate a long block on that street, then jog left onto another dead-end street (Emado Avenue), and continue where you see the trail heading north.

On subsequent visits to Coyote Creek, you may wish to start at different places. Metcalf Road has good access to the trail; it's about three and a quarter miles from the Riverside Golf access. Farther up the trail, Menard Drive allows access, although it lies in an upscale, controlled-parking subdivision that has been built since the new freeway went through. Drive to the end of the road, and you will see the path near a low wooden fence. Parking is problematic.

You will find a truly public access to the trail at Shady Oak Park, on Coyote Road in San Jose. From Coyote Road, skate all the way across Shady Oak Park and look around for a rusty bridge. The trail is on the other side of that bridge. Look carefully, the trail's a little difficult to spot.

North of Shady Oak Park, the path is badly degraded all the way to Hellyer Park by roots bumping up through the surface. Another section of the path runs near Capitol Expressway and Tuers Avenue; it is discontinuous from the rest of the path and therefore little used. It is also awash in graffiti.

Places to Eat

Along Old Highway 101 you can still find some charming places to buy fruit and a bite to eat, including Pedrizetti's Winery at the south end in Morgan Hill. But this area is changing rapidly. Refreshments may be had at the golf course (open at 6 A.M.), and there are many places to shop and eat along Old Highway 101 (Monterey Highway) in Morgan Hill, just south of where the trail starts. The truly delightful time to visit this neighborhood is in the spring, when fruit stands sell local cherries about a mile or two from where you are going to skate.

Public Transportation

You can take the bus to Hellyer Park. Hop on SCTA 72 or 73 from downtown San Jose; SCTA 180 goes from downtown San Jose to Fremont BART.

Other Trails to Check Out in the Neighborhood

The north end of the Los Gatos Creek Trail

Points Beyond

Chapter 28

Santa Cruz's West Cliff Drive

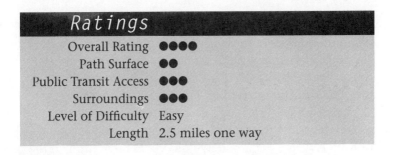

Ratings	
Overall Rating	●●●●
Path Surface	●●
Public Transit Access	●●●
Surroundings	●●●
Level of Difficulty	Easy
Length	2.5 miles one way

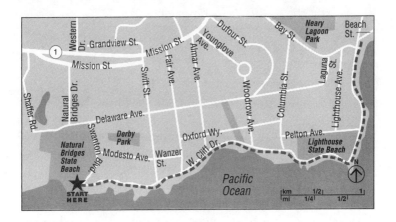

Santa Cruz's skating path attracts skaters, no doubt about that. Maybe not as many as Venice Beach in Los Angeles, but a fair number of skaters, nonetheless. The trail is on the south side of town, next to West Cliff Drive. It starts at Natural Bridges State Beach and runs about two and a half miles along the bluffs above the beach and headlands before ending abruptly at Beach Street. It's easy enough for beginners and curvy enough for experts.

Before the earthquake of '89, the resort town of Santa Cruz was jam-packed during good weather. This engendered expensive parking meters and a somewhat hard-line attitude toward tourists, as if we were something they would always have plenty of. So many people used to come into town and skate around by the amusement park, for example, that the city passed a law saying you can't skate on the roller-coaster side of Beach Street—or in any public park or on the mall, either! Since the quake, though, it's been kind of quiet.

Unfortunately, nobody's gotten around to repealing the restrictive ordinances passed during boom times. The police can still levy draconian ninety-dollar fines for skating on the wrong side of the street. Out on West Cliff Drive, though, there's no problem. And the Pacific panorama, from the skating path on these cliffs, is incomparable.

How to Get There by Car

Take Interstate 880 south through San Jose and follow the signs for Santa Cruz/Highway 17 South. Highway 17 will take you all the way to Santa Cruz.

On the outskirts of Santa Cruz, Highway 17 intersects Highway 1. Take a moment to look at a map so that when you get to this crossing it won't be confusing. Highway 17 turns into Ocean Avenue; this is not where you need to go, even if it is heading in the correct direction. You want to take Highway 1 north, which at this point is heading almost directly west. After about a half mile on Highway 1 north, you will come to a big (for Santa Cruz) intersection, where you need to bear right onto Mission Street. Follow Mission Street several miles (it is the incarnation of Highway 1), and turn left onto Swift Street. Make a right onto Delaware Avenue, then a left onto Swanton Boulevard. Natural Bridges State Beach is on your right. Park anywhere near the end of Swanton. The trail is between you and Monterey Bay.

What It's Like

Natural Bridges State Park marks the western end of the trail. No signs prohibit you from skating into this park, and it doesn't cost any money to skate in (as opposed to entering with your car and parking there). The entrance is a bit steep; the park is a natural wonder.

The trail proper is to your left, along West Cliff Drive. The beach below is part of Natural Bridges State Beach. Take a moment for the view of Monterey Bay and the Pacific. This part of the trail has hardly any traffic noise.

For the next two and a half miles, all you have to do is keep on the path and try not to be dangerously distracted by the beauty of the ocean. Around every twist and turn—and there are quite a few, as the drive follows the coastline—you will encounter a new vista of rocks and crashing surf. Note also the many dedicated overlooks and abstract sculptures. The asphalt surface is getting a bit old and bumpy.

About a mile and a half along the path, you will come to another state beach called Lighthouse Field. It's okay to leave the path and skate around the lighthouse. In fact, the lighthouse is now the Mark Abbott Memorial Lighthouse, which houses the Santa Cruz Surfing Museum. If surfing is a religion, then this is the temple. Skate on in and have a look around.

Outside the surfing museum, the staff of Ski Shop Santa Cruz sometimes holds skating instruction.

As you round the bend from the museum and get back on the trail, you can usually see some surfers and kayakers down below in Steamer Lane, "an internationally renowned surfing site," according to the Santa Cruz Longboard Union.

From the lighthouse to the Santa Cruz Beach, the trail might get crowded with pedestrians. That large hotel-like structure on the right marks the end.

Places to Eat

If you are looking for an interesting place to get some food and maybe a beer, try the Catalyst on Pacific Avenue. You can skate there from the eastern end of the trail, with just a bit of street skating. You will be skating on the sidewalk outside of the first motel you have passed on the beach side (the Sun and Sand). Ahead of you looms the tallest structure in town, the Dream Inn. Continue on West Cliff Drive, which heads toward the small motels across the street. The drive then crosses an unsafe-for-autos bridge spanning the tracks of the Felton and Big Trees Railroad, a wonderful tourist attraction in itself. (The bigger street going off steeply downhill to the right, which appears to be a continuation of West Cliff Drive, is Beach Street.) On the other side of the bridge, you will find a short downhill section (not too steep) and another cheap motel, and then West Cliff Drive ends at the intersection with Pacific Avenue. Pacific Avenue heads off to the right. Skate up Pacific a few blocks—it hooks left a bit—and you will see the Catalyst Cafe on your left. The management says it's okay to skate in and be served. Don't skate on Pacific Garden Mall, which is right around the corner from the Catalyst.

If you had taken Beach Street steeply downhill to the right before that railroad overpass, you could go to Marianne's, a pizza joint at 125 Beach Street. You can skate in; just be careful not to skate on the other side of the street.

Places to Rent Skates

Ski Shop Santa Cruz (408-426-6760) at 124 River Street is easy to skate to; it's just a few blocks from the Catalyst. And get this: one hundred percent of your rental can be applied to the purchase of skates! Lessons available at the lighthouse.

Places to Stay in Santa Cruz

The Dream Inn is a fine place to stay, and it is almost directly on the trail. It has a pool and a hot tub, but the tub is off-limits to kids.

A little more down-home—and you can skate right out of your room—is the Sun & Sand Inn next door, at 201 West Cliff Drive (408-427-3400).

Public Transportation

A bus station in downtown Santa Cruz serves Greyhound and Peerless Stages. It's about two blocks from the Catalyst Cafe.

Other Trails to Check Out in the Neighborhood

For a lot of folks, the Los Gatos Creek Trail will be on the way to Santa Cruz; you will pass right by it as you cruise along Highway 17 through Campbell.

Chapter 29

The Monterey Regional
Recreation Trail

Ratings	
Overall Rating	●●●●
Path Surface	●●; some ●●●
Public Transit Access	●●● (Greyhound)
Surroundings	●●; some ●
Level of Difficulty	Easy
Length	5 miles one way

Before you head down to Monterey, get out your copy of John
Steinbeck's *Cannery Row* and reread the first few chapters
about Doc Ricketts and the bums who caught frogs for him.
The Monterey Regional Recreation Trail starts just across the
city limits of Monterey, in the town of Seaside.

> The owner wanted a dollar and a half and didn't come down
> to eighty cents for three days. The boys closed at eighty cents
> and gave him an I.O.U. which he probably still has. This trans-
> action took place in Seaside, and the stove weighed three hun-
> dred pounds. . . . It took them three days to haul it to Cannery
> Row, a distance of five miles, and they camped beside it at
> night.
>
> from John Steinbeck's *Cannery Row*

The Monterey Regional Recreation Trail runs those same five easy miles along Monterey Bay, past some of the biological niches and habitats that Steinbeck chronicled firsthand. It ends in the town of Pacific Grove at a beautiful little peninsula known as Lover's Point.

How to Get There by Car

The easy way to get to Monterey from Highway 101 northbound or southbound is to take Highway 156 west from Prunedale and go by way of Castroville and Marina on Highway 156/Highway 1. After the town of Marina, you pass the boarded-up remains of Fort Ord. The next little town on your right is Sand City, and the next exit on Highway 1 is Fremont Boulevard in Seaside. Skip that exit, and take the last Seaside exit at Canyon Del Rey Boulevard. Turn left at the bottom of the off-ramp, just before you get to the Monterey Beach Best Western Hotel, and go back under the freeway. After one long block, you will come to Del Monte Boulevard. The trail begins at the corner of Del Monte and Del Rey.

To park, take a right on Del Monte Boulevard, past the Day's Inn Hotel on your left. Take another right past the Comfort Inn on Roberts Avenue, where there is plenty of parking.

What It's Like

Starting from the southwest corner of Del Monte Boulevard and Canyon Del Rey Boulevard in Seaside, head south along Del Monte. On your right is Roberts Lake.

The trail is smooth asphalt paralleling a railroad track. Vestigial tracks lie sometimes to the right of the trail and sometimes to the left. The trail builders also embedded a few commemorative railroad ties in the trail here and there,

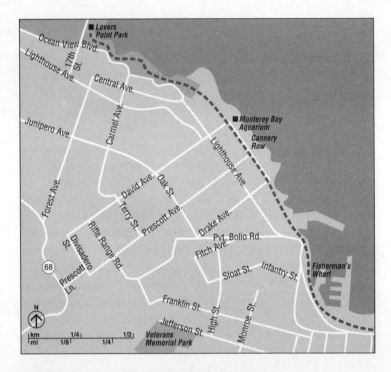

mostly at intersections. This is a nice arty touch, but it can be mightily inconvenient to a skater who trips on them.

Note the Del Monte Gardens Skating Arena on your left. It's open in the evenings several days a week, and for "matinees" on weekends. It's quaint. The cost is about four dollars, "with skates or without." Perhaps the best part is the deco stainless steel winged roller-skate sculpture affixed to the corner of the building. If you want to give it a try, be prepared to take off your skates to get in the door, and then put them back on when you go out on the roll-on urethane-over-wood rink floor. The management says your skates have to be "indoor safe," which means that if they are in-line skates, the nuts and bolts that secure the wheels to the chassis have to have rounded ends.

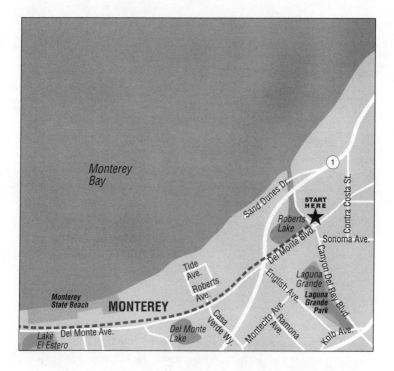

Just past the roller rink you will come to a dead-end road to the right. Take a short side trip along it just so you can say you skated next to a sand dune. The U.S. Government/No Trespassing signs apply to the dunes, not the road.

The trail continues along Monterey State Beach with its sand dunes on your right. When you approach the wharf area, the trail gets a bit confusing, especially at Figueroa Street, where the municipal parking lots are located. If you go to the right here and take the path of pink concrete behind Tony Roma's restaurant, you will stay next to the water and never have to traverse any parking lots. (Take the ramp behind the harbor master's office.) If you go to the left you will skate on a trail next to the sidewalk on the north side of Del Monte Avenue.

By either route, when you approach the plaza by the Custom House, the trail is marked with traffic signs (Recreational Trail). Keep to the left near Fisherman's Wharf; skates aren't allowed on or near the wharf. There is a remarkable bronze sculpture near Heritage Harbor on the other side of the wharf, a life-size hyperrealistic figurative likeness of Saint Rosalia.

A block or two past the wharf area is Cannery Row. This is a concrete trail with several inconvenient cross streets, in prime tourist territory. Skates may be rented at several locations here. The trail runs next to a genuine post office in a genuine Railway Express Agency railroad car. Note Doc Ricketts's Lab, a juke joint right next to the trail. Next door is the Emporia Restaurant and Carousel. The kids are really impressed by that carousel. On the kids' right is a spectacular marine wonderland. If only we could get the kids to be as fascinated with the tidal cycles of life as they are with that magnificent merry-go-round. Try this out on them:

> Doc was collecting marine animals in the Great Tide Pool. . . . It is a fabulous place when the tide is in, a wave-churned basin, creamy with foam, whipped by the combers that roll in from the whistling buoy on the reef. But when the tide goes out the little water world becomes quiet and lovely. The sea is very clear and the bottom becomes fantastic with hurrying, fighting, feeding, breeding animals.
>
> from John Steinbeck's *Cannery Row*

There is wine tasting at 700 Cannery Row. A block or two farther, past some more difficult cross traffic, you arrive at the biggest tourist draw on Monterey Bay, the Monterey Aquarium. Be careful of the cars leaving the employee lot.

The city lights this part of the trail for night skating.

Just past the aquarium, the trail enters the town of Pacific Grove. No more cross traffic. Sometimes it gets crowded; beware of the rented, four-wheeled "bicycles" on the path. The trail ends rather abruptly at Lovers Point Park.

On the way back, when you cross the plaza by the Custom House, you can follow the yellow line to Del Monte Avenue. The trail between Washington and Figueroa has been under construction for years now.

More experienced skaters can skate over to the beach at the beginning of the trail in Seaside. If you go west on Canyon Del Rey Boulevard to the end and turn left on Sand Dunes Drive, you will have arrived at Monterey State Beach, surely one of the loveliest spots on earth you can skate right up to. Note that you are skating past two freeway on-ramps, and the cars are not very kind or understanding.

Places to Eat

When you get to Reeside Avenue, near Cannery Row, head two blocks away from the bay to the Bagel Bakery. Excellent bagels, excellent coffee—a great place to go during an early morning skate.

For later in the day, try a remarkable sports bar in Pacific Grove, called Tavern by the Bay. It's across Ocean View Boulevard from Stanford University's Hopkins Marine Station, just west of the aquarium, in a complex of factory outlets called the Tin Cannery. They will serve you a beer (and some great seafood) at the tavern as long as you are seated. The Tin Cannery allows skates; there is a ramp at the west end of the building.

If you are looking for an elegant restaurant at the end of the trail, try the Old Bath House. It's expensive; in my opinion, it's worth it; and they serve skaters (with their skates off).

Places to Rent Skates

Adventures by the Sea (408-372-1807), on Cannery Row. They also rent kayaks.

Places to Stay in Monterey

You might consider the Day's Inn across the street from the beginning of the trail. It's certainly not as well appointed as the Monterey Beach Hotel located around the corner next to Monterey State Beach, nor is it precisely on the trail, as is the Comfort Inn across the street. However, the Day's Inn is ruggedized for skating; you can skate right up to your room on wide concrete verandas. Day's Inns make a real effort to attract the trade of travelers with kids, so be sure to take advantage of the kids' meals that come free with the room. If you call in advance, you can get a room on the fifth floor with a view of Monterey Bay; if you call a few weeks in advance, you can get room 530, which is at the end of the cell block and where nobody at all walks past your window.

Public Transportation

If you want to get to the Monterey Regional Recreation Trail by public transport, you will be pleased to note that the Greyhound station is right on the trail at Del Monte Avenue and Adams Street in downtown Monterey.

Other Trails to Check Out in the Neighborhood

Coyote Creek Trail in San Jose/Morgan Hill is en route for most readers.

An unnamed trail starts at the bottom of the off-ramp at the northernmost Fremont Boulevard exit off Highway 1. You already saw it as you drove into town. It runs along the freeway for miles and miles. Right next to the freeway, in fact. If it weren't so, this trail would have a chapter all to itself, but situated as it is, it will have to be content with being a footnote.

Chapter 30

The Venice Bike Path

Ratings

Overall Rating	●●●●●
Path Surface	●●●●; some ●●●●●
Public Transit Access	●●●●
Surroundings	●●●●
Level of Difficulty	Easy
Length	7 miles one way

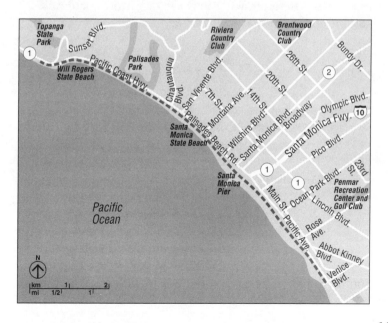

The Venice Bike Path sets a de facto standard for roller-skating paths. You skate all the way from Will Rogers State Beach in Pacific Palisades, down through Santa Monica, past Ocean Park, and almost all the way past Venice Beach—about seven miles. There are no cars; in fact, the air supply is a breeze off the ocean at all times. The trail is flat, smooth, and interesting. It's perfect for kids and beginners, as long as everybody leaves skating room for the flashier skaters.

But the fresh air, great views, and ideal pavement aren't the only things that make this a five-star trail. There's something else special about the Venice Bike Path. You're not an outlier here, you're an accepted part of the culture. If you're a good skater and have good form and a reasonably flashy style, you're appreciated for that.

Venice fits my definition of five stars, "an exceptional skating experience, worth even a long trip, and not to be missed." When you get there, the skaters will gladly tell you about other places to skate around Los Angeles, like Long Beach, Huntington Beach, San Diego's concrete boardwalk, and the Strand on Coronado Island.

How to Get There by Car

Take Interstate 10 (also called the Santa Monica Freeway) west, all the way to the coast, until it becomes Highway 1 (also called the Pacific Coast Highway, or PCH). Go north on PCH to Will Rogers State Beach. Park in one of the public lots on the beach side of the street; they're open year-round and aren't too expensive.

What It's Like

Start skating south on the bike path from Will Rogers State Beach. It's the most recent addition to the trail, so the traffic control is pretty good, with left and right lanes and a few directional signs. After about three miles, the trail links up with a concrete trail that runs along Santa Monica State Beach. For steady exercise, stick to this northern part of the trail; for distractions, continue south. As the Santa Monica Pier comes into view, keep an eye out for a Y in the path. Both forks take you to the same place, but I recommend the left fork, which is straighter. Just after you go under the Santa Monica Pier, you'll see a ramp on the right that takes you onto the pier. You could explore the pier and take the kids to the carousel. There's an apartment above that merry-go-round where a number of famous writers have camped out to concentrate—Tennessee Williams, for example.

Near the ramp is a skate rental place, and down the path a few paces is a well-tended grassy plot. This is a good place for novices to practice. You can rent skates and then learn how to stand up on them on the grass.

South of the pier, the trail segregates into a path for skates and bikes and another path for walkers and joggers. There are some serious skaters out here; it's not a good place to dawdle.

Once you get to Venice, stop outside the Venice Recreation Center, where some of the flashiest skaters on earth dance to music and run the slalom course.

The path comes to an end at Venice Boulevard.

Places to Eat

You can find some dynamite pizza and deli food on the path, just south of Loew's Hotel, near the Venice/Santa Monica border.

Places to Stay near the Beach

Loew's Hotel is right on the path. It's a bit pricey, but it's worth it to be right there on the trail for just a day or two. It avoids the hassles of Santa Monica's Ocean Avenue.

Places to Rent Skates

Not far from the Santa Monica Pier carousel is Sea Mist (310-398-8830), a good rental place if you get there early.

If something goes wrong with your skates, try Jim McDowell's Rip City Skates at 2709 Santa Monica Boulevard in Santa Monica (310-828-0388).

Public Transportation

Several RTD and Santa Monica Blue Bus lines will take you to the Venice Bike Path. The Freeway Flyers can take you there directly from LAX.

Index